P9-ARD-174

COUNTERCOUP

Also by Kermit Roosevelt

Arabs, Oil and History
A Sentimental Safari
War Report of the O.S.S.
The Overseas Targets:
War Report of the O.S.S. Volume 2

COUNTERCOUP
THE STRUGGLE FOR THE CONTROL OF IRAN

Kermit Roosevelt

McGRAW-HILL BOOK COMPANY

New York – St. Louis – San Francisco – Auckland
Bogotá – Guatemala – Hamburg – Johannesburg
Lisbon – London – Madrid – Mexico
Montreal – New Delhi – Panama – Paris
San Juan – São Paulo – Singapore – Sydney
Tokyo – Toronto

Copyright © 1979 by Kermit Roosevelt
All rights reserved. Printed in the United States of America.
Except as permitted under the Copyright Act of 1976, no part
of this publication may be reproduced or distributed in any
form or by any means, or stored in a data base or retrieval
system, without the prior written permission of the publisher.

LIBRARY OF CONGRESS CATALOGING IN PUBLICATION DATA
Roosevelt, Kermit.
    Countercoup, the struggle for the control of Iran.
    1. Iran—Politics and government—1945–
2. United States—Foreign relations—Iran.
3. Iran—Foreign relations—United States.
4. Great Britain—Foreign relations—Iran.
5. Iran—Foreign relations—Great Britain.
6. Roosevelt, Kermit. 7. Diplomats—United
States—Biography.   I. Title.
DS318.R66   320.9'55'05   79-10318
ISBN 0-07-053590-6
    0-07-053593-0 (Pbk)

First paperback edition, 1981

1234567890 SMSM 87654321

Dedicated to

the long-standing friendship between the Iranian and American people and to its continuation, albeit under different circumstances.

Author's Note

I am indebted to many friends and former associates for their help and encouragement in this book, but it seems best for several reasons not to enumerate them.

This book ends in triumph. The Shah, having made a "successful" flight in good Moslem tradition, returned a victor. Ardeshir Zahedi, later to be his son-in-law and later still *ex*-son-in-law, played a "successful" hero's role. (Twice he served as Iranian Ambassador in Washington.) The United States and Great Britain lent "successful" support. At the end of this true account, in the late summer of 1953, the Shah said to me truthfully, "I owe my throne to God, my people, my army—and to you!" By "you" he meant me *and* the two countries—Great Britain and the United States—I was representing. We were all heroes.

Now, I must say sadly, that is no longer true. What was a heroic story has gone on to become a tragic story. In the economic field, in the distribution of land to the peasants, for example, the Shah had moved from success to greater success. He encouraged outside investors to undertake development projects, such as the steel plant near Isfahan, which brought major new sources of income to the Iranian people. The oil and gas pipeline running north into the Soviet Union added substantially to the actual, and to the prospective, economic growth of his country. High-level corruption, endemic in Middle Eastern societies, did "skim cream" off the top. However, the Iranian population as a whole shared in these financial benefits.

But the Shah failed to recognize that from economic success grow a people's political aspirations. The French Revolution followed close upon the peasants' acquisition of additional, even if very little additional, revenue. In Iran there has been substantial growth of revenue and enormous broadening of the educational base. The Shah did not take into account the growth of political ambitions which inevitably followed. Thus he went from economic success to political failure to tragedy.

Now the Pahlavi regime is ended. By Persian standards it was brief. In 1971 the Shah had celebrated the 2,500th anniversary of Persian monarchy. Of that giant span of years, his dynasty lasted for just over half a century. Considering the shortness of their rule, the Pahlavis must be credited with major contributions. The three dynasties—Afshar, Zand, and Qajar—which preceded them together endured less than a century, adding but little to the country's progress. The Safavids, from A.D. 1500 to 1736 by our calendar, had one outstandingly successful leader, Shah Abbas, who reigned from 1587 until 1636. The Pahlavi contribution was second only to his in "modern" Iran.

What will take the place of royal rule is by no means clear. Very possibly the present confusion will end in the establishment of another dynasty, whether the ancient title of Shah is continued or not. Whatever may come, the story I tell here is still relevant—to what has passed and what is yet to come.

Washington, D.C.   K. R.
March 15, 1979

COUNTERCOUP

CHAPTER
1

"Attar has traveled the seven Cities of Love
But we are still at the first corner of the first street."
Jalal ad-din Rumi (d. 1273)

The morning was muggy, close to rain. My anticipation rode high but was accompanied by a nagging dread. On this day, June 25, 1953, our course of action in Iran would be decided. Would we follow the plan on which I had already agreed with the British, tentatively in my mind but decisively in theirs?

I was carrying a twenty-two-page paper that set forth the project. The British had done a draft, which I had rewritten because it was too precise. They had outlined a complete plan; the most I thought we could do was define an objective. True, the paper should look as much like a plan as possible. But I did not want someone, in Washington, London or wherever, peering over my shoulder later on, saying: "Wait! This isn't what you said you'd be doing."

Excitement about the meeting in the Secretary of State's office, scheduled for eleven o'clock that morning, predominated. It was now quarter past ten, and my nerves, I must admit, were not at ease. There was still time, too much time. Speculations, fruitless ones, kept flooding my mind. I thought about the bloodshed that might occur—the frightening consequences of failure, the complications which could too easily accompany success—all these circled through my head as I prepared to seek approval of what had become my full-time preoccupation.

AJAX was the cryptonym assigned to the operation. ("Cryptonym" is defined in my dictionary simply as a "secret name," and the CIA used cryptonyms to identify specific clandestine operations.) What AJAX was intended to be was a cooperative venture. It allied the Shah of Iran, Winston Churchill, Anthony Eden and other British representatives with President Eisenhower, John Foster Dulles and the U.S. Central Intelligence Agency. The alliance was to be formed for the purpose of replacing an Iranian Prime Minister, Dr. Mohammed Mossadegh. Dr. Mossadegh had already attempted to expel his monarch, replacing him with himself, and he had formed an alliance of his own with the Soviet Union to achieve the result he wanted. The wily old man, variously estimated to be between seventy-one and eighty years old in 1953, thought the affair to be his own brainchild. Others saw it differently. The real initiative behind that second alliance came, in cold fact, from the Russians. Many Mossadegh supporters realized this. In recent months the Iranian Communist party—the Tudeh—had strengthened its control over the "Mossadegh movement."

Recognition of that fact, and of the dangers it

presented, was bringing together the U.S., the U.K. and major elements in Iran. These elements, I was convinced, included the Shah, the bulk of the armed forces and an overwhelming majority of the people.

The original proposal for AJAX came from British Intelligence after all efforts to get Mossadegh to reverse his nationalization of the Anglo-Iranian Oil Company (AIOC) had failed. The British motivation was simply to recover the AIOC oil concession. We were not concerned with that but with the obvious threat of Russian takeover.

I took the shuttle bus from "temporary" K Building, constructed (to put it politely) during World War II between the Lincoln Memorial and the Reflecting Pool, which stretches toward the Washington Monument. The bus took me to the CIA headquarters at 2430 E Street, where I was to meet the Director, Allen Welsh Dulles. From there we went in the agency Cadillac to the State Department office of Allen's brother, John Foster Dulles. By the time we arrived, the threat of rain had become a reality. It did nothing for my confidence.

Inside JFD's office an impressive assembly was already gathered. The northern end of the room had a normal-sized sofa with an oblong teak table, covered with ashtrays, in front of it and leather-covered armchairs on either side. Beyond that was the Secretary's gigantic desk at which he now sat, occupied simultaneously with two telephones—not an unusual situation for him. Presumably the calls had nothing to do with the reason for our presence. Beyond him, a long table filled the southern end of the huge room. Here a substantial group was gathered, in respectful silence, to give their serious consideration to our proposal.

At least so it seemed. I soon realized that most of the group had already concluded that anything but assent would be ill-received by its chairman. If "serious

3

consideration" did not lead to approval, it would best be forgotten.

The assembly was a distinguished body of men. They were not, it is true, all distinguished in the same way. The Under Secretary of State, General Walter Bedell ("Beedle") Smith, was, to take one instance, a small, astringent man who looked every bit as sour as he generally was. But he had an aggressive air of authority which conveyed distinction, and we did have the advantage of knowing that he was on our side. He had been Allen's predecessor as Director of the CIA and lived just a block from me in northwest Washington. A year earlier, when he had still been Director, my wife and I had been the owners of two young, aggressive beagles who used to trespass on Beedle's property. At a morning staff meeting he had transfixed me with his steely glare. "Roosevelt," he rasped, "if you can't keep your goddam dogs out of my garden, I'll shoot them!"—and probably you too was the clear implication. I had just discovered what was attracting the beagles. "General, if you didn't have a skunk living under that big azalea bush in your garden, my dogs wouldn't set foot in the goddam place." He frowned, glared, then suddenly gave me a broad grin. The subject was dropped, the skunk evicted, and I later gave away the beagles.

Beedle, as I knew well, was personally inclined to favor clandestine operations. In some respects he was a forthright man—particularly in his choice of language, which could be brutally frank. But in other ways he had a devious mind. To this side of him, covertness, the hidden approach, had a strong appeal. Operation AJAX might, in crucial areas, be suspiciously undefined. Nevertheless it was exactly "his dish of tea," an expression he was fond of using. I was totally confident of his approval.

One of Beedle's deputies was seated next to him, H.

Freeman ("Doc") Matthews, a chunky figure with graying hair, a florid complexion and a genuinely kind disposition. On this particular morning he looked vaguely remote. I took this to mean that he disapproved of the matter we were to discuss but was well aware of the way his two bosses, JFD and Beedle, viewed it. Both were, in his opinion, totally convinced even before reading my paper. Doc would not feel it appropriate to argue against them.

Robert Richardson Bowie, sitting beside Doc Matthews, was a lawyer and, between other assignments, a professor, first of law and later of international relations, at Harvard University. At that time he was director of the State Department's policy planning staff. Later, from 1966 to 1968, he served as Counselor to the Department. Still later, President Carter appointed him a Deputy Director of the CIA. Not normally disposed to keep his opinions to himself, in this case he shared Doc's assessment, both of the situation and of what to do about it: keep silent. His round red face, under a thatch of white hair, was noncommittally bland. The cigar he was smoking contributed to a generally thoughtful air.

At his right, at the end of the table, was Henry ("Hank") Byroade. Since his first ambassadorial post (to Egypt in 1955–56) he has been ambassador to more posts than any other man in American diplomatic history—South Africa, Afghanistan, Burma, the Philippines and Pakistan. At that time he was Assistant Secretary of State in charge of NEA (the Near East, Africa and South Asia, which has since lost Africa to a separate division). He had, unlike many of the others, already read our proposal. He knew the Secretary's views. Accepting the fact that discussion would be useless, he sat in silence, drumming his fingers on a knee, his black brows forming an uncompromising line that matched his equally straight, uncompromising mouth. His opinion did not need to be, and was not about to be, expressed in words.

I was concerned that JFD had not yet applied himself to the paper that had been so carefully prepared. In part, as I have noted, it was the result of conversations with the British. But far more important were the meetings I had held in the Middle East with four of our own key people. None of them was to play any part in the actual operation. Nonetheless—if the damn thing was ever going to be approved—they would have made major contributions to its success. They were all old Iran hands. One had spent the years before and during World War II in the country; he was now chief of the Agency's Iranian desk in Washington. Two of the others were consultants— "cleared" outsiders who also knew the country intimately and on whom we could call for information or advice as needed. The fourth was still my number-one man in the region, though he would be leaving before the operation actually got under way.

Now, to my annoyance, Foster had hung up one phone but was still talking on the other. I resumed my study of the group assembled around me. On my side of the table, at the far left, was Ambassador Robert D. Murphy, who was Deputy Under Secretary for Political Affairs. I had known him since World War II, when he had been in charge of clandestine preparations for the Allied landing in North Africa. This operation, TORCH, had represented a major contribution to the first really big Allied victory of the war. When he died on January 9, 1978, Chalmers Roberts wrote in the *Washington Post:*

Bob Murphy was one of those civilian soldiers of a period in our history now remote to new generations of Americans. He was a pillar of the conservative State Department establishment, rising to the top posts held by careerists. He believed in "standing up to the Russians" or to Hitler or any other totalitarians. Yet there is nothing I have ever discovered in the record to show that, when his government acted in ways he thought unwise, he attempted an end run or leaked a decision to prevent its implementation. In history's light he may at times have been wrong, but he was a loyal and highly competent servant of his country.

Thus Bob Murphy was, of the State Department people present, the only one with any experience in undercover operations—and his had been an outstanding success. But he, too, was silent, noncommittal. Unlike most of his colleagues, however, he did give me a friendly grin and a feeling that he was, even if only faintly, sympathetic.

Next to him was the Secretary of Defense, Charles ("Engine Charlie") Wilson, ruddy-faced, white-haired and cordial in a gruff way. There was a military aide, whose name I can't remember, between him and Ambassador Loy Henderson, who sat next to me. Loy was, without question, a key person in the meeting. He had rushed to Washington from his post in Teheran for the express purpose of offering his recommendations. JFD might decide, but Loy would be most influential in that decision.

Loy had been first an acquaintance of mine, then an increasingly close friend, ever since the early days of World War II. For a brief period during that war I had worked for Dean Acheson while he was Assistant Secretary for Economic Affairs. Loy was then in charge of the office concerned with our recently acquired ally, the Soviet Union. Loy had served in Moscow before the war. He knew the Russians well; he distrusted them profoundly. I encountered him later when he was Ambassador in Baghdad, and after that in New Delhi. Nothing he had seen caused him to modify that distrust. Now I had been meeting with him in Teheran while assessing the prospects, and later making preparations, for our proposed operation.

Loy's position was clear—and clearly unhappy. A gentleman himself, he preferred dealing with his foreign colleagues in a gentlemanly fashion. But Henderson was one of a small band of distinguished foreign-service officers of that era who understood the realities of life in this world we live in. He feared that Iran under the leadership of Mossadegh was slipping under Russian control. He believed that this would be a grave blow to the West and would constitute an eventual danger to U.S. national security. I doubt that he was ever really optimistic about our prospects of success, but he saw no other course that offered equal hope. He gave our proposal his thoughtful and deliberate support.

Foster Dulles was finally finished with his telephones. He got up from his desk and settled himself at the head of our table, with brother Allen on his right and me on his left. Picking up the thick paper which had been placed in front of him, he looked casually around the group and said, "So this is how we get rid of that madman Mossadegh!"

The remark was met with silence and, in some cases, barely concealed flinching. Beginning to read, he was soon flicking the pages with considerable speed, leading one to wonder how carefully he could be reading. Every now and then he would put a question to Allen.

In many respects Allen was a gray edition of his brother. In fact, he was younger and, despite his mild manners, no less forceful. But his appearance and often his behavior were deceptive. His large leonine head, gray mustache and twinkling gray eyes, his booming laugh (Foster's had a rasp to it that Allen's lacked), his voice, generally low but occasionally, in moments of feeling, quite high-pitched, and perhaps most of all his periodic attacks of gout—which he did not allow to interfere with a strong game of tennis—all distinguished him from the apparently harder, tougher Foster. Now, as his brother asked him a question, Allen would refer it to me and I would answer in the fewest words possible. My objective was simple: to get the paper approved as quickly as could be done and to get out of the office immediately thereafter.

So I sat nervously on the edge of my chair and answered Foster's questions, each one referred to me by Allen, as well and as confidently as I could. I was well aware that there were skeptics even among the relatively few in the CIA who had knowledge of the project. In all cases these were men who knew the intent but not the content of this paper. But otherwise, from Allen on down, enthusiasm and confidence ran high. That part of the plan which concerned the Iranian military had been checked out most discreetly with the Pentagon. To the best of my knowledge it had met with enthusiastic backing. The Secretary of Defense himself was generally, probably very sketchily, informed. He was, however, appropriately enthusiastic at this meeting, and we did welcome his support.

Allen and I were, of course, aware that most of the assembled group were strongly pro-Israeli. So one of the points we emphasized—separately, together and as often as possible—was that Iran was *not* an Arab country. It did, in fact, have excellent though informal relations with Israel. These relations became closer in later years when certain Israeli friends discreetly joined the CIA in helping to organize and give guidance to a new Iranian security service.* This informal Israeli action was entirely "under the table," essentially

*See an article on William Colby, former Director of the CIA, speaking to students at Utah State University. "Colby said the CIA created SAVAK, the Iranian police force [sic], and taught it proper methods of intelligence."— Logan (Utah) *Herald Journal*, November 10, 1978.

a clandestine operation—but it was of great value to the Iranians.

Eventually, when Foster Dulles had flicked the last page over, he leaned back in his chair, pushed his glasses up on his forehead and looked, this time, at me.

"Kim," he drawled, "for the benefit of these people, some of whom have not had the chance to read your paper, I'd like to let them have some idea of the importance of Iran. After that, why don't you give us just a brief summary of how this thing is supposed to work out?" His flat voice sounded almost as though he were bored, going through the motions to include those around the table in his decision—which, clearly, he had already made.

"First, you gentlemen do know, I assume, where Iran is and what it is." He was now speaking to us like a schoolmaster. "Persia, as it used to be named, has been throughout history the bridge between Far Eastern Asia and the lands of the Mediterranean and Europe. Although her importance as a trade route declined after the construction of the Suez Canal in the 1860s, her strategic location has made her a bone of contention among great powers—always Russia, often France and Germany, now Great Britain and, by association, the United States.

"Today it covers an area of over six hundred thousand square miles. This is a lot less than it has been, for nineteenth-century wars lost her considerable territory. But Iran is still called an empire and her king the Shahanshah, or 'King of Kings.' The 'empire' lies between the Caspian Sea on the north and the Persian Gulf on the south. It has common frontiers with, running west to east, Turkey, Iraq, Soviet Russia, Afghanistan and Pakistan. Looked at in another way, being tucked up against the southern border of the Soviet Union, it does block Russian access to a warm-water port. Of course they have the Black Sea, but this is separated from the outer world by the Bosporus and the Dardanelles. These are held by the Turks, a cantankerously independent-minded people on whom the Russians have learned not to rely. If they could control Iran, they would control the Persian Gulf. This has been their dream, their chief ambition, ever since the days of Peter the Great. That was," he noted dryly, "a good many years ago, about two and a half centuries.

"In closing, I would like to emphasize what has already been pointed out. Iran is not an Arab country and its relations with Arab neighbors, particularly Iraq, have often been most troublesome. So we do not want to confuse the issue with worries about Israel. Israel must be as interested as we are in keeping the Russians out of Iran. And, of course, most Arabs are too.

"Now, over to you, Mr. Roosevelt." He bowed, half mockingly, in my direction.

I took a deep breath. "Sir," I began, "we have, as you know, studied this situation very thoroughly. You remember that the British first approached us before the election, before President Eisenhower and you were in office. Naturally, the British have been primarily concerned with their oil problem, while our concern has been principally the Soviet threat to Iranian sovereignty. On Mr. Allen Dulles' instructions I have been to Iran several times to make assessments. The last two times have been since the election. I would say that we are now satisfied about the major questions that concerned us. First, the Soviet threat is indeed genuine, dangerous and imminent. At this moment, time seems to favor the Russians and their unwitting ally, Dr. Mossadegh. My second point seems almost contradictory, but I am equally convinced about it. That is, in a showdown that is clearly recognizable as a showdown, the Iranian army and the Iranian people

11

will back the Shah. They will back him against Mossadegh and, most especially, against the Russians. To my mind there is no doubt about that.

"So we are now asking your approval to move ahead. As you do know, we have British approval. As soon as we have yours, we can communicate with the Shah himself, which we have not felt free to do as long as we lacked the final U.S. go-ahead. We hope we will have that this morning."

Foster Dulles nodded his head almost imperceptibly and gave a small grunt which I took to indicate his approval so far. A door opened across from the Secretary's desk, wafting the scent, to put it politely, of Bob Bowie's cigar in my direction. I waved it away as Foster dismissed the interruption.

"Let me now summarize the way we view this undertaking. From the outset I should make it plain that what we have is no more than a projection of what might happen. We do know that the Shah wishes to replace Dr. Mossadegh. But we have not yet felt able to confer with him. There is no way of foretelling in advance how things will develop, so what we really offer now is an objective, a hope, a goal. This paper outlines one possible course to that goal. We do feel confident that we can achieve it, but we do not wish to mislead you into believing that, as of now, we can tell you exactly how.

"One point is central: This can only be a *joint* undertaking, with the fullest cooperation from Iranians under the confident, enthusiastic leadership of the Shah himself. Unless we can achieve such understanding, such commonality of purpose, the success we and the British seek can never be achieved. The British cannot work in Iran at all, and it would be fruitless for us to try to work alone. Everything I say from here on is based upon the achievement of a trust and a true working alliance between the Iranians and ourselves, with the British contributing as much support as they can.

"The first objective naturally is, with the Shah's backing, to organize the military support. We would propose to contact carefully selected army leaders. I repeat, 'carefully selected.' The present chief of staff, General Riahi, is a key supporter of Mossadegh. We are not exactly sure how many of his subordinates have also shifted their loyalty from their proper Commander in Chief, who is by law the Shah himself. There are, of course, some. But in the showdown we are seeking, very, very few would cling to Mossadegh and Riahi against His Imperial Majesty.

"On the question of Mossadegh's replacement, we have had strong indications that the Shah's choice is General Fazlollah Zahedi. The British have reservations about him. That is putting it mildly, for they held him a prisoner in Palestine during World War Two. But we know and trust him. Zahedi is presently in hiding after Mossadegh attempted to have him arrested. His son, Ardeshir, is a young man well known to some of our embassy personnel. They have complete confidence in him. He is brave and absolutely loyal, not only to his father but to the Shah as well. He will be an invaluable, completely reliable contact with the general.

"There are other officers and civilians who can play important roles. These are men in whom we, the Shah and our British friends who will be watching and helping from afar have complete confidence. If we get approval from you now, the next step will be to get the Shah's agreement. After that we will work with him to line up sufficient strength for him to act. Once he dismisses Mossadegh from office and names Zahedi to take his place, there must be prompt support for his action. Together we must organize the necessary military and popular backing which will make any resistance from Mossadegh and his ally, General Riahi, absolutely hopeless. And if that can be done, the Russians also will find it hopeless—impossible to intervene.

"We are quite satisfied, sir, that this can be done successfully. All we wait upon is your decision."

Before Foster could say anything, Allen interjected a swift suggestion. "Kim, you had better cover two more points before the Secretary comments: first, on the estimated cost, and secondly, I think you should give your idea of the 'flap potential'—what could happen if things should go wrong."

I could feel myself redden as I realized that of course Allen was right. I should have covered both points early in this discussion.

"On the cost, sir, we really feel that it will be minimal—at least minimal for anything of such vital significance. One, or perhaps two, hundred thousand dollars is the most I can see us being required to spend.

"Your second question is very difficult to answer. I have already said that if we get all the support I have outlined, I see no prospect of failure. If we have badly misjudged the situation, the consequences are hard to gauge. The least one can say is that they would be very bad—perhaps terrifyingly so. Iran would fall to the Russians, and the effect on the rest of the Middle East could be disastrous. But I must add this: These are the same consequences we face if we do nothing."

"All right. I think you have made the prospects clear, alarmingly clear. Now, over to you," said Allen, nodding to his brother.

Foster Dulles sat silently for a moment, twiddling a pencil in his thick fingers, his lips compressed and brow furrowed in thought. Then he looked directly at me and plucked a name—how I do not know—out of the air.

"What about General Guilanshah?" he asked and grinned faintly at my surprise.

"You evidently know, sir, that he is commander of the air force. There is no question of his absolute loyalty to the Shah. But we see no role for the air force in this undertaking. We want to keep knowledge of our plans to the smallest possible number. Therefore we have no present intention of being in touch with General Guilanshah."

There was a momentary silence—thoughtful or confused, depending on who was contributing to it. I went on.

"There are some other people involved. First, as you know, British Intelligence, since the English were expelled from Iran by Mossadegh last year, have established communication for us with their principal Iranian friends. They may well have some important contacts they do not think it necessary to reveal. But at least they have put us in touch with two men whom they think could be of the greatest use. These are known under pseudonym as Nossey and Cafron, and I shan't identify them further. In fact, I have not yet met them, but the British are very high on them, recommend them strongly. Even though there will be no British in Iran during the operation, the people we are working with, some of whom you have met, include Mr. Cochran, a very senior man in their Intelligence who is in charge of the operation for British interests. His two principal lieutenants are also involved. One of these, Gordon Somerset, was their chief man in Teheran until the British got thrown out. He has been helping us contact a few of his good Iranian friends now outside of Iran. The other is Gordon's boss, Henry Montague, who is going to be stationed on Cyprus to provide the radio contact between those of us who will be in Teheran and those of you remaining in the outer world."

Dulles smiled faintly but said nothing.

"On the American side, our principal area director, George Cuvier, will be leaving shortly after I get there. He has really become too prominent a feature of the local landscape to stay on during this kind of an operation."

Also, though I did not add this, he had told me quite frankly that the upcoming occasion as we planned it was, to use Beedle's expression, just "not his dish of tea."

"His successor-to-be has been in the Middle East for almost a year. You may recognize his name—Bill Herman. At the time of the Azerbaijan crisis of 1946–47 he was covering it for one of our major press syndicates. We wanted someone who had a background in the country free of Agency connections. Although he has been with us for several years, he has not been back in Iran since the late Forties. We have a couple of other first-class people already in the embassy there, and I am taking one of our paramilitary people with Far Eastern experience—a man named Peter Stoneman—to be our principal contact with the local military. He is a good, tough character and his background should impress the men he'll be working with.

"Then there are two nationals I should mention who have already proved themselves in this preoperational stage. They will, I am sure, be extremely valuable in the weeks to come. They are brothers whom we refer to as the Boscoes. They came to us on their own, absolutely out of the blue. We have checked them every way we can. Although they quite frankly refuse to disclose some of their background experience and even some of their present associates, we are satisfied. They have already proved themselves in one action, which I would prefer not to discuss at this time. But we are confident we can count on them to turn out the bazaar in support of H.I.M., and that will be all the signal needed by the people and the army."

At this point I could not think of anything further to say. What in the world would we—more specifically, I—do if the Secretary did not approve the operation? How could we get the British to understand? Would they give up gracefully? I did not see how they possibly could. But if they did not, what action was open to them? They could not work alone in Iran when they could not even get their own people into the country. They would be furious, frustrated and unpredictable. I got another whiff of Bowie's cigar and had to fight a sneeze. Foster Dulles was still silent. Other desperate thoughts flooded my mind. What if he approved and we failed? That was something I had thought of often and had satisfied myself, absolutely, that we could not fail. There was no possibility. But . . .

Finally Foster looked directly at me. He raised his bushy eyebrows, as if acknowledging that I had said my say. Then he nodded gravely and glanced away from me to survey the others at the table. "Well, let me have your comments—if any," he said gruffly. "Begin with you, Allen."

Allen spoke very briefly, with proper lawyer's ponderosity. In sum, he felt that the project had been adequately, not to say thoroughly, studied. The British had made their contribution and our own most knowledgeable officers, in the Agency and in other concerned departments, had given all possible help. One could not deny that there were risks, but he was confident that they could be overcome and that we would succeed.

From him Foster proceeded counter-clockwise around the table. Most people simply grunted, signifying consent with the least possible commitment.

Beedle, as usual brief, also sounded, as usual, surly. "We should proceed. Of course!"

Doc Matthews and Bob Bowie simply shook their heads, more up and down than across, a little on the positive side of noncommittal but not much. Hank Byroade, at the end of the table, spoke almost inaudibly, certainly unenthusiastically, but nonetheless to be understood as supporting the proposal. Farthest to my left was "Engine Charlie," inarticulate as usual but enthusiastic. He was supported by a nod from the military type next to him. Then it was Loy Henderson's turn. He did not hesitate but spoke gravely, firmly.

"Mr. Secretary, I don't like this kind of business at all. You know that. But we are confronted by a desperate, a dangerous situation and a madman who would ally himself with the Russians. We have no choice but to proceed with this undertaking. May God grant us success." Folding his hands across his chest, he leaned back in his chair and looked upward, as if soliciting the Deity's assistance.

So finally it came to me. "Sir, I think this simply has to be done. It is impossible to be sure, but for some reason I *am* sure. We can do it."

The Secretary gave me a quick grin and got up immediately.

"That's that, then; let's get going!" He walked over to his desk, picked up one of the telephones and waved us from the room. I hoped that perhaps he was calling the White House, that he was making an appointment to get the President's concurrence. But I never knew.

Certainly it was with mixed feelings that I left his office. On the one hand, it was good to have our project approved. The manner of its acceptance to my mind implied not only support of the Shah but also confidence in the Agency—and in me personally. This I had to regard as flattering. On the other hand, this was a grave decision to have made. It involved tremendous risk. Surely it deserved thorough examination, the closest consideration, somewhere at the very highest level. It had not received such thought at this meeting. In fact, I was morally certain that almost half of those present, if they had felt free or had the courage to speak, would have opposed the undertaking.

But perhaps that is the way government works and why from time to time it fails. Certainly Foster Dulles was to see his share of failures in his time, often for just that reason. I could not know that then. What I did know was that our small group at the Agency had done its preparation thoroughly. And the British, from burning desire more than judgment, were all for the operation. The next step was to find out what the Shah thought.

At any rate, from that point forward, I was on my own. And that, I felt, was not a bad place to be. I could count on maximum support with, in all probability, a minimum of interference. I had a good team with me, a fine venture to tackle.

CHAPTER
2

"Bring me my Bow of burning gold!
Bring me my Arrows of desire!"
William Blake (d. 1827)

When I left Foster Dulles' office with his gruff approval ringing in my ears, I had hoped to be able to hop a plane to Beirut immediately. From there my plan was to drive with Jim Gabor, a colleague stationed in the Middle East, over the mountains to Damascus. Then, to avoid the heat, we would cross the desert at night to Baghdad. In that hot and dusty city we could rest at a mutual friend's house and leave for Iran via Khanaqin. The entry to Iran should be easy. The border guard at Khanaqin would not, I was sure, inform Teheran of the arrival of one Kermit Roosevelt until long after I would leave the country. And since I would be using a discarded cryptonym as my pseudonym* while there, it could make no difference then. Once past the border, we would overnight at Kermanshah or, if we made very good time, at Hamadan, even closer to Teheran. That would get us to Bill Herman's house in the mountains north of town by midday. Bill was my "man in the Middle East," and I would stay with him, his wife Jane and their two children, William, Jr., and Kate, in their comfortable compound—they had a swimming pool, which was a great joy—on a little *koochi*** off one of the main roads.

However, my departure was delayed by an unexpected complication. My annual physical exam, a requirement strictly enforced, was due. The Agency doctor discovered a kidney stone that he thought should be removed immediately. A surgical operation that would interfere with AJAX—at that moment in history—was unthinkable. I got Allen Dulles to overrule the doctor. Nonetheless, I was held up for several days.

But it did give me a final opportunity to review the arrangements we had made. I did not expect to appear in the open, so there were no "cover" plans. I would meet only those people with whom I had to deal directly in connection with the operation. I was to use as pseudonym the operational cryptonym I had used earlier—James F. Lochridge. This had been abandoned when we thought it had fallen into the hands of an Indian woman whom we suspected of Soviet connections. Operationally ambitious, our man in the area had entertained her at his house. When she had gone he could not find the paper on which my name and cryptonym were both, for some reason he could not satisfactorily explain, written together. Some months

---

*A cryptonym is a name assigned for use in "secure" communications. A pseudonym is just a plain false name.

**Persian for "lane."

later he found the paper behind a cushion in his easy chair, so it was still "secure." But I had by then acquired a new cryptonym. Lochridge was still available for my use in any way I wished.

The other most important arrangements included an agreement that Ambassador Loy Henderson would *not* return to Iran until the operation was completed. No embassy personnel—only the small CIA group and, of necessity, the communications officer attached to us—were to know anything of it. Our office was quite apart from, though near, the embassy. Matt Mason, the Counselor (number-two man) of the State Department, was an old friend of mine. It would be difficult to keep my presence secret from him, but I was confident of his discretion. He might wonder, eventually even guess, what was up. But he would ask no awkward questions.

The final, vital issue was one of communications. We decided that even the EYES ONLY diplomatic traffic, addressed, say, to the Secretary or the Under Secretary alone, was almost necessarily seen not only by a number of communications people in the Department but also by their top assistants. We could not set up any more secure system without arousing just the suspicions we were seeking to avoid. Anyhow, Allen and I felt that the British should be allowed to make some sort of meaningful contribution to AJAX. So we requested that they assign Henry Montague to Cyprus—a damn good idea it proved to be—where he could receive, and transmit to, me through secret channels all messages relating to our undertaking. Gordon Somerset, until recently a top agent in Iran, who knew many key Iranians personally, had already made one potentially valuable, actually fruitless contribution. The British, of course, received the proposal with greatest enthusiasm. Before I actually left Washington, Henry was already in place, and the radio links had been satisfactorily tested.

When I finally did get on a plane, with my kidney stone still inside me, I had my first moments of relaxation since many weeks before the meeting in Foster's office. The flight was a letdown. There was nothing important I *could* do. I couldn't even concentrate on reading, so I held a book on my lap and, discouraging conversation with my neighbor, let my mind wander. There were plenty of places where it could wander! But I tried to set myself goals. First I decided I could quite usefully review the physical geography of Iran and its neighbors. That might even be classified as useful wandering.

The first incident that came into my mind was a day in late September 1941 when General William ("Wild Bill") Donovan called me into his office. He was then Coordinator of Information—chief of what was known as the COI. (This was later split into the Office of Strategic Services—OSS—which he headed, and the Office of War Information—OWI—under playwright Robert Sherwood.) I had been one of Donovan's earliest employees because—my Ph. D. thesis being on "Propaganda Techniques in the English Civil War"—I had written an article on the kind of clandestine service organization the U.S. should develop for World War II. When I showed the draft to my cousin, columnist Joseph Alsop, he had immediate advice.

"Don't publish it. Bill Donovan is an old friend of your family's, isn't he?" I nodded. "Then send it to him. FDR is authorizing him to set up something very like what you're proposing."

I followed his suggestion and had a prompt reply from Donovan. "Do *not* let your piece get into print. Come and work for me instead. It won't be for a couple of months, but by August we'll be in business."

One morning in late September, Donovan summoned me to his office. Pearl Harbor was still three months away, but he was absolutely certain that somehow we would be drawn into war. I shared his feeling.

I cannot now remember just what he wanted, but I do remember that as I was leaving he called me back.

"Kim," he asked, "what do you think of happenings in Iran? That's going to be an important part of the world for us."

At that point, I must admit, I had very little to contribute on Iran. I knew roughly where it was but little more. So I said, safely but noncommittally, that "it looks serious." That was satisfactory for the moment. As soon as I was out of his office I looked up Iran in an atlas and an encyclopedia. Thereafter I kept myself better informed.

This early commitment affected the whole course of my life. A few weeks after I joined Donovan another family friend suggested I go out to China with him to work for General Claire Chennault. I was tempted but felt unable to accept. (What would have become of AJAX if I had gone to China?) Instead, I went first to the Middle East, including Iran, and ended up completely fascinated by the area.

One thing I did immediately after the Donovan interrogation: In addition to consulting the atlas and encyclopedia, I visited a colleague at the Library of Congress. Ralph Bunche, later Under Secretary General of the United Nations, was already doing research work for the COI and well able to answer my questions.

Ralph was a quiet, studious-looking black gentleman who received me with appropriate gravity.

"Kim," he began, "I take it I'm to start from scratch." I nodded and he went on: "First, the Middle East, as you call it, stretches from Algeria on the west, across northern Africa through Egypt, Palestine [as it was then, for the state of Israel did not yet exist], Lebanon, Syria and the Arabian peninsula, all the way to Afghanistan and India [the relevant portion of what was then India is now Pakistan]. Iran, Afghanistan and India are *not* Arab. Don't ever confuse Iranians with the Arabs. They don't like it.

"Friends or not, they snuggle together south of eastern Turkey, Soviet Azerbaijan, the Caspian Sea and Russian Turkmeniya. Actually Iraq is wholly bounded by Turkey on the north; it is Iran that lies against the Soviet Union.

"Now to give you some idea of comparative sizes: Iran is four times larger than Iraq—about six hundred thirty thousand square miles to something over one hundred forty thousand for Iraq. To compare it to American or European standards, look at it this way. Texas, our largest state, is around two hundred sixty-six thousand square miles. This makes Iran two and a half times larger than Texas. And Iran is larger than West Germany, France, Spain, England, Wales and Scotland combined. That's a lot of territory. Does that give you some sort of picture?"

After a bit of comparative cogitation, I agreed that it did.

"Iran's really a hodgepodge of contour and climate. The north, along the Caspian coast, is—" he hesitated to search for an apt comparison—"rather like Indonesia. That probably doesn't help you much." I agreed. "They grow tea along the side of the hills; there are mulberries and silkworms closer to the shore."

I was suitably impressed and said so. But I was sorry that I did not then know Indonesia—I made my first trip there some seven years later—to be able to make the comparison.

Dr. Bunche continued: "The Elburz mountains north of Teheran are topped by Demavand at eighteen thousand six hundred feet. They run into Turkey and the Russian Caucasus. The Zagros range curves southeast along the Iraqi frontier, turns farther east and goes down to the Persian Gulf. The peak, or rather the rounded dome, of Demavand has a fringe of snow all year round. The upper slopes of the higher Elburz and Zagros mountains are white-capped from fall to spring. But the interior, south of Teheran to the Gulf and east to the Afghan–Indian border, is generally warm to hot—and *very* dry. There are two major deserts, in fact, the Dasht-i-Kavir, running from a bit south of Teheran due east almost as far as Meshed, which is one of the big shrine cities, and southeast to join up with Dasht-i-Lut, which continues to Baluchistan and the Gulf coast just to the west of India.

"In nineteen thirty-eight, which was about the last complete year of 'peace' before friend Hilter invaded Czechoslovakia, the Middle East produced more than ten million tons of oil per year. If it's any easier for you to understand, that is more than eighty million barrels, or three billion three hundred and sixty million gallons! Almost all of that came from Iran."

"Sounds like a lot, doesn't it?"

"In terms of the way world consumption can be expected to grow, it's not all that much. But it is a lot, even assuming that much more will be discovered. More important, it is obviously not an endless supply." The professor shrugged his shoulders and moved on to happier subjects.

"Particularly in or on the edge of the Zagros range are some of the most famous and loveliest cities of Iran—Qum, another pilgrimage center; Isfahan, 'half the world' to earlier Persians; and Shiraz, home of two of the greatest poets of Islam, Saadi and Hafiz. Of course you remember the famous encounter between Tamerlane, the Mongol conqueror, and Hafiz?"

I acknowledged that I did not. Ralph looked disapproving. Surely as a Harvard graduate (Ralph himself had a Ph. D. from Harvard and taught there before joining the U.N. staff) I must know *something* about Persia.

"Well, Hafiz had written of his Shirazi sweetheart, 'I would give Bukhara and Samarkand for the mole upon her cheek.' These were the cities that Tamerlane called home. When he seized Shiraz, Hafiz was dragged before him. His verse had got around.

"Tamerlane was not a gentle type. He was even known to carry on the venerable Mongol custom of making pyramids from the skulls of conquered people. He looked at Hafiz and thundered: 'Miserable wretch, I subjugate continents to adorn Bukhara and Samarkand. You would sell them for the mole of a Shirazi wench!'

"Hafiz, who had been living in poverty, looked pointedly at Tamerlane's gorgeous garments and then at his own rags. 'Sire,' he replied, 'it is through such rash spending that I have fallen on these evil days.' The story goes that Tamerlane was so pleased by this answer that, instead of punishing Hafiz, he rewarded him liberally.

"There is one further point you should understand. Let me ask you a question: What *are* Persians?" Ralph did not wait for an answer. He was sure I could not provide one. "By no means are all of the inhabitants of Iran called Persians, Irani or, to put it more properly, Aryans. The 'Iranian' population"—he looked at me over the top of his glasses, every inch the professor now—"descends from the early Aryans who moved into the region about fifteen hundred B.C., give or take about five hundred years. The people already there, known as Caspians or Caucasians, intermarried with the 'new' arrivals and were absorbed by them. In the seventh century A.D. and the centuries after that, Arabs moved into the west and particularly the southwest. From the tenth century on, for several hundred years, 'Turkish' tribes were also coming in. These 'Iranian Turks' have little racial affinity with the modern 'Ottoman' Turks. They came originally from central Asia, and many of them still speak a Turkish dialect called Azari. The Qashqai tribe—whose language is very close to Azari—probably migrated from northwestern Iran to the South-central area where they now live."

I did not then realize how well and under what awkward circumstances I was to come to know the Qashqai. So I said nothing.

Bunche continued: "Almost all the inhabitants of Iran are Moslems, over nine tenths of them Shiah; the remainder, mostly Kurds, are Sunni.* There are small numbers of Armenians, Jews, Parsis or Zoroastrians and Christians—Nestorians and a very few Protestants and Roman Catholics. And that's about it. That is Iran."

I thanked Ralph for filling some major gaps in my education. When Donovan next spoke to me of Iran, I was quite knowledgeable.

That concluded my geography review for the trip. I turned to history. The Pahlavi dynasty, which then ruled Iran, was comparatively new. Reza Shah had been the founder, starting as a young Cossack colonel who had expelled Russian advisers with British support. A few months later, in December 1920, he seized

---

*The Sunni, or Sunnites, are the majority Moslem sect who accept the authority of the Sunna, the oral tradition of the Mohammedans. The Shiah, or Shiites, give more status to the traditions of Ali, the prophet's nephew who fled from Iraq into what is now Iran. Most western Moslems—Arabs, Turks, North Africans—are Sunni. Many of the eastern Moslems, mostly Iranian but Afghani, Pakistani and Indian also, are Shiah.

Teheran without any warning to the British. General William Ironside, the senior U.K. officer, awoke one morning to find Reza in control. That evening the young Shah Ahmed Qajar named Reza's ally, Sayed Zia-ed-Din Tabat-Abai, to be Prime Minister, and Reza was appointed Chief of Staff. The sayed, growing ambitious, did not last long, and Shah Ahmad was encouraged to "study" in France. (He never saw Iran again.)

In the fall of 1925 a Constituent Assembly deposed the Qajars and named Reza regent. Elections were called, a new assembly named, and on December 12, 1925, its 280 members unanimously proffered the crown to General Reza Khan. To nobody's surprise, he accepted. And, sixteen years later, in September 1941, his son succeeded him.

The details of this succession are, to put it mildly, relevant to my story. In fact, they mark the real origins of AJAX.

These go back to the Anglo-Russian occupation of the country in the summer of 1941 when the second year of World War II was close to an end—before the Japanese attack on Pearl Harbor added another hemisphere to the action—and the fighting had spread from the Mediterranean shore deep into the Middle East. British concern over German activities there had been growing for some time. After the Nazi invasion of the Soviet Union, the Russians added their complaints. They claimed to have evidence that the Germans were planning a *coup d'état* in Iran. In mid-July the U.K. and U.S.S.R. sent Teheran a note of protest, which they followed with an even stronger note on August 16. Nine days later force took the place of notes.

Simultaneously, the Russians from the north, the British from the south and west struck sharply into Iran. Their armored columns took the meager defense forces by surprise. Air strikes in the south wiped out

Iran's small navy; soldiers were heavily bombed in their barracks around the capital. Before the Allies could reach Teheran, a week after the first strike, the Shah's Prime Minister resigned. His successor sued for peace. Even though he had accepted Allied demands, the Anglo-Soviet forces announced that they would occupy Teheran on September 17. If their intention was to give the old Shah notice and time to abdicate, they were successful. On September 16 Reza Shah Pahlavi turned over the throne to his son Mohammed Reza, then a month short of his twenty-second birthday.

His Imperial Majesty Mohammed Reza Shah Pahlavi, Aryamehr, Shahanshah of Iran, as he became officially known, was a slim, dark young man. His future was, in most estimations, decidedly uncertain, as, again in most estimations, he himself was an unknown quantity. In fact, however, he was not so much uncertain as understandably cautious, reserved, quietly inscrutable. He could not afford to be otherwise. The photographs of this time give him a melancholy air, not inappropriate to his circumstances. He was soon to meet three of the four most important men in the world (the fourth being Adolf Hitler), and he was to break through their preoccupation with important matters of war. With each of them—Churchill, Stalin, Roosevelt, in the order of their meeting—he established personal understandings, though of very different kinds. Two of the three leaders were dead by the time of AJAX—Stalin died only a few months before—but all three were important to its development and history.

Winston Churchill, Prime Minister of Great Britain, first came to Teheran in the summer of 1942. On his way to Russia and his initial encounter with Joseph Stalin, Churchill stopped in Teheran for several days to break his trip. The Shah invited him to lunch and he accepted, offering H.I.M. his first heady exposure to discussion of global strategy. During the course of their talk, Allied plans for the invasion of Europe came up. The Shah suggested that the Allies strike Italy first, consolidate there and then stage a massive blow through the Balkans— "the soft underbelly" of Europe, as Churchill later put it. "No doubt it was," observed the Shah, "a coincidence that our minds had met in the same broad strategic conception. Had the plan been followed, the subsequent history of central Europe would clearly have been very different."*

Later, the Americans—President Franklin Roosevelt, General George Marshall and Admiral William Leahy—insisted on Normandy when they, too, came to meet in Iran. This was at the then famous, now largely forgotten, Teheran Conference. It occasioned the one and only visit there of "Cousin Franklin," as my family addressed him, but better known to the world as FDR. The conference, involving him, Churchill, Premier Joseph Stalin and peripherally the Shah, lasted from November 28 to December 1, 1943. Having one meeting with Churchill already under his belt, the Shah was quick to bring his own personality and the problem of his country to the attention of the principals in attendance. He met separately with each of them, and these meetings, apart from their historical significance, have a direct bearing on my story.

The fullest account was written by the late Ambassador Charles E. ("Chip") Bohlen, who described the preliminaries and the conference itself as having had, on him at least, a substantial impact.** (His fluency in Russian was responsible for his being involved.) He

*Mission for My Country, London: Hutchinson & Co., 1961, p. 79.
**Bohlen, Witness to History, New York: W. W. Norton & Co., 1973.

started by recounting the flight from Moscow to Cairo for a pre-Teheran meeting. This was made in the ambassadorial plane, a converted B-25 bomber, of Averell Harriman, chief of the U.S. mission to the U.S.S.R. Harriman was later, in the company of General Vernon ("Dick") Walters, to play a significant role in the events leading up to AJAX. His companions, an assortment of American and British officials, must have been exceedingly uncomfortable if my own experience in B-25s is any guide. As they neared Stalingrad the pilot reported engine trouble. He put down, and while mechanics tried to find out what was wrong the passengers were taken to the Communist Party headquarters for a sumptuous lunch with—true to Russian hospitality—large quantities of vodka. A tour of the battlefield followed, which Bohlen confessed he could not remember very clearly. On returning to headquarters they found an even more substantial banquet with even more vodka. Bohlen entertained the group by singing a Cossack song about the hero of a seventeenth-century peasant uprising who threw his Persian girlfriend into the Volga River. This amused the Russians and possibly edified any of Bohlen's traveling companions who could understand it.*

Meanwhile, from Cairo the Harriman plane accompanied FDR's larger craft to Teheran on November 27, landing at the airport south of the city. Driving into town, the party found the road lined with people, which led them to worry about security measures. It had been planned that the President would stay with the American Minister in his relatively unguarded quarters. This would require him to drive daily through totally unguarded streets to the Soviet and British embassies, which were close together. Soon after the Americans had settled in the Minister's

*Ibid., pp. 134–35.

residence, Molotov told Harriman that Soviet intelligence had uncovered a plot among Nazi-oriented Iranians to work with German agents infiltrated for the assassination of one or more of the principals in the conference. Therefore Stalin was offering FDR a building to himself in the heavily protected Russian compound, where meetings could be held in safety. Churchill had no reason for worry. His legation— it became an embassy immediately after the conference—was guarded by a regiment of Sikhs. Bohlen said that although FDR was "skeptical about the plot," he accepted the offer. On November 29 he moved into the building Stalin had assigned him. Bohlen himself was quartered at Amirabad. His job in Teheran, he commented, was "the hardest sustained period of work I ever did."*

The Shah has described his meeting with each of the principals:

Stalin was particularly polite and well-mannered, and he seemed intent upon making a good impression on me. He went so far as to offer me a regiment of T34 tanks and one of fighter planes, and in view of our desperate shortage of modern arms I was most tempted.

But a few weeks later, when his offer was stated in more specific terms, some onerous conditions were laid down. Russian officers and NCOs would have to come with the gifts. The Russians alone would decide where the tanks and planes would be located, the tanks to be based only at Qasvin [to the west and somewhat north of Teheran] and the planes in Meshed [close to Iran's northeastern frontier with the U.S.S.R. and Afghanistan]. Until the end of a training period whose duration was not specified, both the tanks and the planes were to be under the direct command of the Russian general staff in Moscow. It was as if the military advisers, who are today helping us strengthen our army, were to tell us, "Your army must be under our

*Ibid., p. 138.

command, or we shall give you no aid!" Of course, I could not accept old Joe's offer, any more than I could approve a similar proposal from any other country. I declined with thanks.*

The first encounter with Stalin created suspicion and mistrust in H.I.M.'s mind. These feelings were dramatically magnified by the Azerbaijan crisis three years later.

The Shah noted that "for some strange reason" President Roosevelt stayed at the Russian embassy, where Stalin was also staying. "Roosevelt's physical disability of course made it difficult for him to move about, but it seemed a curious situation that I had to go to the Russian embassy to see him, while Stalin came to see me. All the conference sessions were also at the Russian embassy, except for a birthday party which Churchill gave at his legation."**

In the only conversation he had with the Shah, FDR was particularly affable. He showed great interest in the reforestation of Iran as a means of protecting agricultural land against the encroaching desert. Once his presidential term was over, he told the Shah, he would love to return to Teheran as an adviser on reforestation. The Shah had the impression that FDR was joining the ranks of distinguished Westerners who had become fascinated by his country and its culture. While the President and he disagreed profoundly on some points of foreign policy, the Shah found him admirable in other ways and was "only sorry that his untimely death prevented his following up his welcome suggestion."***

The Teheran Conference settled the issue between Churchill on the one hand, FDR and Stalin on the

*Mission for My Country, p. 80.
**Ibid., p. 79.
***Ibid., p. 80.

other. The Allies would invade Normandy, not the Balkans. Beyond that, H.I.M.'s efforts to get the three wartime chiefs to make a declaration of policy concerning Iran had this much success:

> The governments of the United States of America, the U.S.S.R., and the United Kingdom recognize the assistance Iran has given in the prosecution of the war against the common enemy, particularly by facilitating the transportation of supplies from overseas to the Soviet Union. The three governments realize that the war has caused special economic difficulties for Iran and they agree to make available to the Iran government such economic assistance as may be possible. . . .
>
> The governments of the United States of America, the U.S.S.R. and the United Kingdom are at one with the government of Iran in their desire for the maintenance of the independence, sovereignty and territorial integrity of Iran. They count upon the participation of Iran, together with all peace-loving nations, in the establishment of international peace, security, and prosperity after the war, in accordance with the principles of the Atlantic Charter, to which all four governments have continued to subscribe.[*]

The declaration may not have fully satisfied the Shah. Averell Harriman refers to it without mentioning any FDR meeting, or discussion of a possible statement, with the Shah. "A declaration on Iran also was signed at the last possible moment. This brief document . . . was dealt with casually at Teheran, although it assumed considerable importance in the first postwar crisis over Azerbaijan."[**] At least H.I.M. had achieved this most valuable objective.

Since that time I had been personally much involved in the local history. My own first trip to Iran was early in 1944, a bit over three months after the Teheran

---

[*]Quoted in *ibid.*, pp. 80–81.

[**]Averell Harriman and Elie Abel, *Special Envoy to Churchill and Stalin: 1941–1946*, New York: Random House, 1975, p. 282.

Conference. A curious concatenation of events had taken me to Egypt first and thence to Iran.

Bill Donovan had sent me to Cairo in January 1944, principally at the request of Dean Acheson, then Assistant Secretary of State for Economic Affairs. The obligation to Acheson arose in this fashion. A friend of mine had recommended to me, and I in turn to Dean, one James Landis* to be senior American Economic Minister in the Middle East. This was an important job. It affected our relations with Middle Eastern countries, especially as it bore on relations with our major allies, the British. Landis, in spite of everyone's best efforts, insisted on regarding the British, not the Germans, as his principal enemy. Word of this got to London, then to Washington. Acheson spoke to me sharply.

"Kim, you are responsible for a madman, a raving lunatic, being my chief representative in a key theater of this war." The usual faint twinkle was not to be seen in Acheson's blue-gray eyes. "Now I am going to make the punishment fit the crime. Bill Donovan has agreed that you can go to Cairo for both of us until this mess is put in some decent order. After that, Donovan can do with you what he will. But until then, you haul your tail out there and sort things out!" Despite his sartorial elegance and "correct" appearance, Dean was given to salty language when he thought salt suited the occasion. And he was grimly determined that, despite Mr. Landis' peccadillos, the Middle East must be a *British* area of responsibility.

So I hauled my tail to Cairo to sort out a mess which I could not regard as wholly of my making. But, clearly, I was stuck with it. The Landis problem took

---

*Landis had been in charge of civil defense in northern California in the days after Pearl Harbor, when many feared that a Japanese attack on the U.S. West Coast was imminent.

some time to resolve; meanwhile, I had an interesting and often enjoyable time. First, I wangled my way to Jedda, my introduction to Saudi Arabia, which was almost to rival Iran and Egypt in my postwar life. Soon after that an expedition to Iran was organized. Making use of my OSS responsibilities, I talked myself aboard the airplane but remained part of the economic mission as "cover." Such are the advantages of having two bosses; no one can know for whom you are really traveling. So Landis, a handful of economic people from his staff and the mysteriously undefined I took off for Teheran.

My first flight to Teheran was a beautiful one. We flew in via Habbaniya, the airfield south of Baghdad, where one of many German attempts to break into the Middle East had recently been thwarted. (A rebellious Iraqi, Rashid Ali, had called for Nazi help. His Iraqis, and the small contingent that was all the Germans were able to send, had been defeated by British General Glubb Pasha and the Jordanian Legion, which had marched swiftly across the desert from Amman to take them by surprise.) After our Habbaniya halt we headed over a range of mountains that grew higher and higher as we approached Teheran. They peaked to the north with Mount Demavend, which, as Bunche had told me, does rise over 18,000 feet. We interrupted our hearts game to whistle in appreciation.

"God damn," said Landis, "that *is* a mountain." He was absolutely right. There were great patches of snow in the lower, wooded ravines and sheltered hollows of the upper rock. Demavend towered aloofly above the lesser heights, wearing its white with dignity. If it were reduced in scale, there would be nothing of impressive beauty about the mountain, but hugeness and distance give it great majesty. Today Demavend is harder to see because of smog enveloping the rapidly industrializing capital, but when it can be seen it is still overpowering.

We stepped from the plane onto the airfield, surrounded by a semicircle of mountains and a low, sprawling city. Again, Landis was moved to speech, this time by the Red Army soldiers guarding the field. "Look at those cute toys they've got. Little submachine guns with ventilation, no less!" The guns had an outer metal sheath with holes so that they could still be held after the barrel had heated. I was more impressed by the rows of Lend-Lease planes on their way to the Soviet Union and by the American army vehicles marked in three languages with three different alphabets—English, Persian and Russian. It was really educational.

Landis and I were lodged in Amerabad, an army camp a few miles northwest of the airport, where Bohlen had earlier stayed. Our quarters were in the comfortable senior officers' billets, and we ate at their mess, which was a great convenience. Inevitably I was making comparisons with Cairo, an ancient citadel crowded with appurtenances of modern war, and Jedda, still a small town mostly within its old walls. So Teheran struck me as an extremely up-to-date city, which was the intention of the former Shah, Reza Pahlavi. He had torn down the handsome wall (until this century Middle Eastern cities were generally walled for security) and widened the streets by the simple expedient of removing anything that happened to be in the way. Thus, most of the buildings along the main avenue were only about fifteen years old. On some of the streets you could still see houses that had been sliced in half so that the streets could be broadened. Nonetheless, much of the old remained, including a lovely mosque next to the Majlis (Parliament) building. This itself has a Persian-style garden—that is, one with trees, pools of water with fish swimming in them and fine rosebushes. The rosebush by the palace was the largest I had ever seen.

A unique feature of Teheran is its location. High mountains stretch across the northern limits, rising as high as 14,000 feet; to the northeast, topped by Demavend, they are even higher. The southern edge of Teheran—then the bazaar, now far south of that—was more or less flat. At an altitude of 4,000 feet the ground rises as the city progresses north. What were in those days small hill villages have now grown into residential suburbs, stretching up to an altitude of 8,000 feet. Until a few years ago the Royal Teheran Hilton, built in the early 1960s, was on the northwest limit. Now there has been much building to the west and even to the north.

Iran had a dreamlike quality to it. The first few days were spent talking with our legation staff and the Millspaugh* economic mission people. I was also able to crowd in some sightseeing. The bazaars were the first covered ones I had visited, Jedda's being open, the Damacus and Aleppo *souks* (Arabic for "bazaars") as yet unknown to me. Joseph Upton, one of the men I had come especially to see, represented New York's Metropolitan Museum of Art. He escorted our group through the excellent museum of Persian antiquities, explaining as we went the Met's arrangement with the Iranian government. The New York museum undertook the diggings and excavations, sharing the find with Iran on a fifty-fifty basis; items were divided by Joe into two equal groups, the toss of a coin deciding who got which.

After the guided tour Joe Upton and I had a private meeting so that he could fill me in on developments of

*Arthur C. Millspaugh wrote *Americans in Persia* (Washington, D. C.: The Brookings Institution, 1946) to describe his mission.

interest to the OSS in recent months. His summary was both more inclusive and more specialized than that given me earlier by Ralph Bunche.

"Operationally, so far as the war is concerned, this country is almost as important as any of the fighting fronts. It is *the* key to Russian survival. Whether," he added skeptically, "we are always going to be grateful for Russian survival is another question.

"A certain amount of support has reached the U.S.S.R. via the north by sea, but shipping losses are fantastically high. The bulk of the aid that the Russians use to fight, to survive, reaches them by ship through the Persian Gulf to Abadan and then on by rail to Azerbaijan. From there they take charge, but up to that point it is our responsibility. And where the hell do you think they'd be without the essential supplies we move to them—through this country?"

He thought for a further moment. "The Iranians may have even more cause to regret this than we will." Then he shrugged away his somber appraisal.

"You know of the German attempts to break into the Middle East?" I nodded. "OK, let me give you the strategic layout of Iran. You understand the importance of the western border, running north from Khorramshahr—above Abadan, where the railroad begins—through Kermanshah to Lake Urmia and Tabriz. Julfa, where the Russians take over responsibility for the supplies, is due north of Tabriz. The railroad runs more or less northeast from Khorramshahr, through Dizful and Qum to Teheran, then northwest to Kazvin, Mianeh, almost to Lake Urmia and then due north through Tabriz to the Soviet border.

"The Caspian Sea, which stretches about three hundred miles east to west about a hundred miles to the north of Teheran, you can pretty much forget about. The mountain passes are blocked by snow much of the year and very tough going at any time. You couldn't possibly get through now. When the snow lets up the fog rolls in. Ground travel is unpleasant, and flying—to put it mildly—is risky.

"You might try to get to Azerbaijan, but I don't think you'd ever get the necessary permits. The most interesting place you could go is south, to the Qashqai country." I pricked up my ears, recognizing the name I'd heard from Ralph Bunche. "But I doubt if you could get as far as Shiraz, which is where they'd be now. Why don't you see if you could wangle a plane ride to Isfahan? That's the upper edge of Qashqailand, and even if they aren't there it is lovely—definitely worth a visit."

I said I would try. His final suggestion was that I talk to our other OSS colleague in Iran. This man, he told me, had far longer experience there than he or any other American.

That colleague was a Yale professor by the name of Roger Black. Roger spoke Farsi fluently and was then teaching history in Teheran. He was a testy character, often pithy with words, at other times discursive to an exhausting degree. I found him interesting enough at the time. Half a dozen years later he was to prove much more than that. Roger reported that two Iranian brothers, knowing of his OSS connection and suspecting him of similar affiliation with the CIA, had approached him with a proposition. What they had in mind would later develop into operation AJAX. Fortunately, when Roger turned them over to me, he did so without asking any awkward questions.

I also visited the old palace while in Teheran. It now serves as a museum rather than a residence. On the outside it is most handsome, and the interior is so rich that it takes your breath away as you enter. The rooms are set with mirrors, multifaceted, which catch the light on ceilings and walls. There were tables crowded with presents the royal families, earlier ones as well as Pahlavis, had received over past generations. The rugs impressed me as magnificent; the thrones, of which there are a number, magnificent *and* fascinating. There is an excellent collection of paintings, most by European artists but some of the best by contemporary Persians. We went also to Banque Melli, the National Bank of Iran, to see the justly famous crown jewels and countless bars of gold. The fine emeralds and rubies, great quantities of diamonds and some enormous, perfectly matched pearls are fabulous.

This was all killing time, no more. What I was anxious to do was to follow Joe Upton's suggestion of exploring Isfahan. Curiosity drove me, but curiosity often turns out to serve most useful purposes. I could not know then that Isfahan would be of great importance to me nine years later, and I do not know now why I felt so drawn there. For whatever reason, I sought every possible means of getting to that city "half as old as time."* Finally I latched on to one of our military who had the two essential attributes—curiosity and access to an airplane. The plane was available for only one day, and we could fly only in daylight. But an early start and a late return would give us about six hours there.

The Isfahan landing field underlined the chanciness of the whole undertaking. Hills, which I would have called mountains in Egypt, Saudi Arabia or at home, made the flight bouncy, but the most frightening one rose straight up from the end of the runway. Landing, we pulled up short of its base, but taking off we had to bank so sharply to avoid it that, from where I was

---

*The poet was referring to Petra, now in Jordan, but it applies very well to Isfahan.

sitting, I could not see the sky at all. However, the fabulous attractions of the town—which is now surrounded, though discreetly, by steel mills and manufacturing plants—made my day there the high point of my first visit to Iran.

Driving from the airport into the city, crossing the old stone-arched bridge, I recalled that a British officer, author of an exciting book on his travels in Russia,* had just arrested a "pro-German" Iranian general there. (Many Iranians were labeled pro-German by the British and Russians simply because they were against the occupying powers.) The general's name was Fazlollah Zahedi. The name had no meaning for me then, but I was interested in the story and it stuck in my mind. Years later that name was impressed upon me in ways that have made me—to put it mildly—unlikely to forget it. Meanwhile, there was much else to occupy my attention.

Isfahan had been the capital of Iran for close to three hundred years, from the time of Shah Abbas, about 1600 A.D., till the late nineteenth century. As the old Persian saying has it, "Isfahan is half the world." Its main square is the second largest anywhere today. The largest is the Red Square in Moscow, which I had seen in the summer of 1934, just before starting my freshman year at Harvard. There had been an anniversary or an important funeral or some such occasion. Whatever it was, I had somehow made my way into the reviewing stands. I still remember most vividly the square, with the Kremlin walls and Lenin's tomb behind me, St. Basil's Dome to my right, the Moskva River just out of sight to my left. Columns of marching men and clattering tanks, horse-drawn artillery and aircraft zooming overhead—I could still see and hear

*Fitzroy Maclean, *Escape to Adventure,* Boston: Little, Brown and Company, 1950.

them clearly. But in a different way, the *midan* in Isfahan is just as impressive and even more beautiful. On the west there is a building with an open gallery three floors up from which the early Shahs used to watch polo. In fact this is where the game was first played, with several hundred riders on each team. To the south and east there are huge mosques, and the bazaars begin on the north side. The southern mosque is one of the great sights of the world. Its tiles and mosaics are brilliantly colored, sharply defined, with blues predominating over mixed yellows, reds and greens. And the domes are magnificent, both from outside the mosque and from within, where you can look up and lose yourself in a second sky. In the courtyard, surrounded by mosaic walls and gateways, the bright blue of the real sky is dramatically beautiful.

We went also to another mosque, not on the main square, which is totally different. The walls are plain uncolored bricks of what looks like dried mud. But they are arranged in fascinating patterns. I cannot explain why the result should be so effective—but it is.

At that time, too, there were still old-fashioned rug factories where one could watch little girls working on huge frames which held the vertical threads. Through these the girls wove threads of different colors horizontally, from a platform that was elevated as they progressed. They worked very rapidly, at least while we were watching. Their youth shocked us. It was no surprise to hear that they earned something under thirty cents a day.

Our final visit was to an opium factory. The authorities were already trying to cut down consumption and would issue ration cards only to certified addicts. The cards were emblazoned with a skull and suitable inscriptions warning, in what seemed to me mild language, that opium is bad for you. The factory was directed by a young American member of the Millspaugh mission who told us with some amusement that his mother was president of the Women's Christian Temperance Union in his home state. He had never mentioned to her just what his Iranian assignment was. The place where they processed the opium was not all that interesting, but from there our interpreter took us to a dismal hole where they squeezed the poppies to get their juice. We had to go down extremely narrow alleys. Since the streets were covered and dark it was hard to tell whether we were in a house or on the street. Finally we descended a pitch-black flight of steps and knocked on the door at the bottom.

The door finally was opened by a grimy Iranian in tattered shorts and shirt. He, three assistants and a camel were operating the factory. The factory consisted of a large high-ceilinged room with only one tiny window. In the center there was a millstone rigged up on a pole, and the camel, by trudging around in endless circles, operated the mill. The camel was a huge, shaggy beast, and I couldn't see how they had gotten him into the building, nor how they kept the poor creature there. We were told that they got a fresh camel every two or three hours. I think they must have suspected that we were ASPCA inspectors, because that was obviously absurd.

The millstone was used only for preliminary grinding. The real pressure was provided by a huge block of wood on which a beam—hanging more or less securely suspended parallel to the ceiling—would be brought to rest. This extremely heavy beam was controlled by a complicated system of pulleys and crude gears. When the man wanted to lower the beam, for instance, he went through a fascinating maneuver that involved the insertion of a long pole into the master wheel, which was solid, without any spokes. Then another man released the catch, allowing the beam to move down about two inches. If the beam were to do this all at once, the whole building would collapse, so to absorb the shock the four of them hung onto the end of the pole as it rose miraculously and gracefully to the ceiling. Then they climbed down like monkeys to repeat the performance all over again.

When I returned to Iran, and Isfahan, in 1947, I looked again for this opium factory, but it was no longer there. Strict controls over manufacture of opium were being enforced by the government. Years later, however, I was introduced to opium smoking by Nossey and Cafron* a year after the British had turned them over to me to assist in operation AJAX. I can't say that I was a successful consumer. I smoked, inhaled and got nothing but an occasional fit of coughing. Perhaps the amount was too small, perhaps I was resisting the effect as I later resisted a hypnotist when experimenting to see if hypnotism could be operationally useful. (I had my doubts.)

On our last full day in Iran, we drove up into the mountains north of Teheran, heading for a lead mine called Shenshak about forty-five miles away. We had a day off, and although nothing memorable happened, it was spring, which was happening anyhow, and the mountains, which had happened already. We passed a caravan with tall, ungainly camels and, tagging along at the rear, several donkeys with bright embroidered saddlebags. Having just left town, the caravan was getting itself organized for a long trip, the men scurrying up and down along its sides. We followed the main road, which ran beside the caravan trail and headed

*Pseudonyms. The two, whom I was on my way to meet, were classified in my mind as "agents" working for British Intelligence.

to the mountain through bright hills of sand. The flat plain was soon hidden behind, and the confluent curves of sand, sparsely dotted with young green shoots, eagerly sought by the scattered herds, closed in around the world. Beyond were the mountains, which rose black, bare and forbidding. It was hard to believe that there was life in any of them.

We came to a large fast-moving stream, and the road curved along, climbing some distance above it. Between us and the stream the earth fell in a series of inclined planes. It looked marvelously fertile, covered with pale-green glistening grass, slim erect willows, pears and almond trees with delicate pink-white blossoms and tender young leaves. Above them we could see patches of snow and water trickling down narrow stream beds or gushing from an occasional spring. The hills above, as well as the land below, were cultivated; yellow, pink, purple and light-blue wildflowers, scarlet clumps of poppies added splashes of color to a composition already full of colors—the rich red-brown of exposed earth, the laminated grays of granite, rusty dark ferrous rocks and greenish-black basalt, the sharp white of snowfields and churning water and the frosty blue sky. We passed through one big village of flat-roofed dwellings made of earth and stone, and then the road—always narrow—grew even more narrow and twisted in tightening curves. We finally reached an altitude which we were told was about 10,000 feet, although peaks still rose above us. The mine itself was not all that exciting, but we found a spot out of the wind where we could look back at the way we had come. We clambered around rocky ledges and up sharp inclines until we reached snow—coarse, granulated snow which we quickly packed into solid missiles. We hurled a few at some of the rocks below us before returning to the car. Then we began our long descent back to Teheran.

I am sure it never crossed my mind at the time, but later I should be most grateful for the rough terrain in the north, the edge of which we had just seen. I could confirm what Joe Upton had told me: This was no country for tanks or any kind of armored vehicles. A convoy of jeeps could get through but would be restricted to narrow passes and highly vulnerable to attack. So a Soviet invasion by sea from Baku would be most difficult. Land attack from the northwest, Armenia or Russian Azerbaijan through Tabriz, or from the northeast, Ashkhabad to Mashad, would be more time-consuming. The world would have a chance to respond. But at the moment I was concerned more with Landis than with the Russians.

The Landis problem was resolved only by his recall to Washington in late 1944. It was December by the time his future, *not* to involve the Middle East, was settled. Donovan sent me to Italy, which was uncomfortable, interesting but not as much fun as the Middle East. Just after V-E Day a jeep accident brought me home. I did not return to Iran until the summer of 1947, my longest absence from that country between my first visit and the present day.

One final note: Herbert Hoover, Jr., who was to be deeply involved as State Department consultant and then Under Secretary of State in late 1953 and 1954, passed through Cairo on his way to Teheran in the fall of 1944. We met through a mutual friend at our embassy. He wanted to pay a quick visit to Ethiopia. So did I. Fortunately, I was able to wangle a small bomber from our commanding general in Egypt, and we had a fascinating trip. Hoover went on to Iran, concerning himself, at Secretary of State Cordell Hull's request, with possible oil concessions. The Russians were demanding one in northern Iran, and the U.S. was alarmed that this might be a shield for intentions to annex the area. Thus our acquaintance with each other and with Iran began. The intensity, and the drama, were to come later. But even now one could recognize the factors which John Foster Dulles was to emphasize in June 1953. Not that I was fully aware of all of them—for example, the importance of Iran's geographical location to the world power struggle. But the stake that Russia had there, and the opposing interests of the U.S. and the U.K., were becoming recognizable.

The scent of conflict to come was already in the air.

"On what wings dare he aspire?
What the hand dare seize the fire?"
William Blake (d. 1827)

I cannot pretend that on my flight to Beirut in mid-July 1953 I recalled these events in quite such detail. And I do not know either what detail I omitted. I know that I had lots of time to think—air trips took *forever* in those bygone days—and that I did a great deal of remembering.

The first postwar crisis that came to my mind was one that I observed only from a distance. It developed soon after the German surrender in Europe when, according to the agreed timetable, Allied forces were to be evacuated from Iran. On schedule, American and British troops began to withdraw. But the Russians, in the north, made no such move. The Shah was by now profoundly distrustful of the U.S.S.R. His worries grew ever more intense while Russian ambitions, at the same time and speed, grew ever more clear. Potential conflict developed into actual confrontation. From 9,000 miles away I watched, fascinated, hypnotized—and unable to reach the scene myself.

Two things held me from it. The first was the jeep accident in Italy just after V-E Day; it hospitalized me for almost a year. While recuperating I did some writing for *Harper's* magazine that took me back to the Middle East as soon as I could travel. But one other commitment kept me home. I had agreed to direct preparation of the wartime history of OSS. Written, at Defense Department insistence, in the most horrible officialese language, it took nine months to complete. Until it could be "birthed" I was constrained to be an interested but necessarily distant observer of Iranian happenings.

These were significant, all too often exciting. Ahmed Qavam, who had been Prime Minister in 1942, was again P.M. By mid-February 1946, nine months after V-E Day, British and American troops had withdrawn from Iran. But the Russians, as Herb Hoover and I feared, would not budge. In the northeast, in Azerbaijan, they were arming the Tudeh party, an "independent" Communist party. Soviet intentions were clear: The Tudeh was to set up what would in effect be a puppet state. To establish what they claimed to be self-rule, in August 1945 they had staged a revolt. When the Shah sent loyal Iranian troops to suppress them, the Russians refused to allow his army access.

For the remainder of the year and into 1946, the Russians held on. The date set by agreement with their allies for withdrawal of Soviet forces came and went, with no sign of action. In fact, that spring the Russians actually reinforced their troops in Azerbaijan, increasing tension. They also reorganized the

Tudeh and gave it the innocuous name of the Democratic Party. They had already proclaimed the autonomous republic of Azerbaijan and named as Prime Minister a Communist, Jafar Pishevari, who had spent much of his life in the U.S.S.R. With the aid of Russian arms, equipment and personnel, he established a police state. Then he embarked on a reign of terror.

Hussein Ala, Iranian representative to the newly created Security Council of the United Nations and also Ambassador in Washington, protested before the Council against the Soviet action. His speech, made without instructions from Prime Minister Qavam but certain to have the support of H.I.M., was the first complaint ever submitted to the Security Council.

In the face of total Soviet intransigence, the Shah now turned to the Western Allies for support. U.S. Secretary of State James Byrnes responded affirmatively. Ernest Bevin, his British opposite number, suggested breaking the deadlock by calling a conference of U.S., U.K. and Soviet representatives which could settle privately the questions of Azerbaijan and Kurdestan. This matter came up at the Foreign Ministers' conference in Moscow in December 1945 but was not resolved. The Russians, H.I.M. reported later, "went ahead as if nobody cared."*

In mid-February 1946 Prime Minister Qavam went to Moscow. The Shah, concerned lest Qavam give away the whole northwest of his country, sent his twin sister Princess Ashraf also to Moscow to call upon Stalin. The princess has described this visit: "When the Kremlin gates closed behind me, my heart sank to my boots. I was entirely alone. They had insisted on that. After a long wait in a sinister room, an officer finally appeared. 'Follow me,' he ordered. He took me down a long deserted corridor, then another, then still

*Mission for My Country, p. 116

another. I thought to myself: 'Down there, at the end, they're going to arrest me and I'll disappear forever. . . .' Then, suddenly, a door opened and I caught sight of a man with a mustache, standing with his hands on his desk. It was Stalin. I thought he would be big, broad, terrifying—a real Cossack. What a relief! Stalin was soft and fat, but above all, he was small!"

Ashraf conveyed the Shah's feelings strongly and effectively. The Soviet Premier listened in silence. But when the princess prepared to leave, he suddenly spoke. With a gruff laugh he told her that he had not thought an Iranian capable of such passion. As he sent for an aide to escort her from the Kremlin he said: "Look at that tiny little woman. She's a real *pravda* [a true patriot]." When she left Moscow, Ashraf received a fur coat addressed to "Princess Pravda."[*]

But the situation in the north nonetheless continued to worsen. On March 3, 1946, Soviet forces started moving out of Tabriz in three columns. The first moved toward Teheran, the second toward the Iraqi frontier and the third toward the Turkish frontier. Prime Minister Qavam responded to this move by offering concessions. "He agreed to recommend to Parliament the establishment of a joint Russian-Iranian oil company (the Soviets to hold 51 percent of the stock) to exploit the oil resources of northern Iran; to grant three cabinet posts to Tudeh party members; to recognize the rebel Azerbaijan government; and, finally, to withdraw Iran's complaint against Russia before the United Nations."[**] But at the United Nations, when Ala received the Prime Minister's instructions, and knowing that he had the Shah's total support, he decided to defy them. He refused to withdraw Iran's

---

[*]Gerard de Villiers, *The Imperial Shah*, Boston: Little, Brown and Company, 1976, pp. 126–27.

[**]*Mission for My Country*, p. 116.

complaint from the Security Council agenda and made what has been described as one of the most brilliant presentations in the annals of the Council. This was on March 21, 1946. Five days later Soviet Ambassador Andrei Gromyko dramatically announced at another Security Council meeting that all Soviet forces would be out of Iran in a matter of weeks. By May 9 they were, indeed, all gone.

However, the Soviets continued to give full physical and moral support to the secessionists in Azerbaijan and Kurdestan. In the fall Hussein Ala began to pay a series of calls on Dean Acheson, who was Acting Secretary of State in the absence of Secretary Byrnes. As Dean told me a year later, he believed that the principal role in the Middle East should be, on the Allied side, played by the British. Now, joint action was indicated. Ambassador Ala wanted the United States to take the initiative in reopening the Iranian case in the Security Council. In October 1946 Acheson responded to this point by replying that we could not act *for* but only in support *of* the Iranian government.* That government must initiate the action. Furthermore, he observed, it seemed a mistake to hold elections before Iranian authority was re-established in the province. Then, indeed, United Nations observation and support would be meaningful.

"At this juncture," the Shah has reported, "I followed my conscience. I ordered my troops to Azerbaijan to put down the rebellion once and for all. At the same time I personally flew over the rebel positions to ascertain their strength. The Russians now completely deserted their puppets, and the rebel government collapsed as our forces triumphantly entered Tabriz on 15 December, 1946."

---

*Dean Acheson, *Present at the Creation,* New York: W. W. Norton & Company, 1969, p. 197.

The Shah goes on to recollect an earlier incident of "those eventful days." The Soviet Ambassador urgently requested an audience. When he appeared, he began to speak in threatening tones, protesting Iranian military moves which, according to him, would "endanger the peace of the world."

"You must withdraw your troops *immediately!*" he said with force. As an afterthought, he did add, "Your Majesty."

But the Shah replied coolly, confidently, "Mr. Ambassador, I do not think you understand what is going on in Azerbaijan. Until a very short time ago, what was happening there did indeed 'endanger the peace of the world.' But that, I am glad to tell you, is no longer the case." Although I was not present, I can imagine the flicker of a triumphant smile upon the Shah's face. "The rebel forces have offered their unconditional surrender to my governor general in Azerbaijan. I have his telegram right here."

And he handed it to the stunned Ambassador. As the Shah wrote later, "apparently he had not yet received the news. Unable to think of anything to say, he departed."*

This was the crucial test for the Iranian government. News of the Shah's decision had already reached the common people of the north, and they began to defy the Pishevaris. Even before he spoke to the Russian Ambassador, and secure in his knowledge of the "unconditional surrender" of the rebel forces, the Shah had ordered Iranian troops to move onward. On December 8, 1946, the Pishevari regime was outlawed by royal decree, and on the tenth the Shah's troops captured Mianeh and marched north. Popular uprisings occurred in Tabriz, Rezaieh and eastern Azerbai-

*Mission for My Country, pp. 117–18.

jan. Both the Pishevaris and the rebellious Kurdish regime, though they had been promised Soviet aid, found themselves abandoned. On December 15, as earlier noted, the liberating army entered Tabriz and Rezaieh amid welcoming throngs. Qavam remained on as Prime Minister, and his new party, the Democratic Party of Iran, benefited from the Tudeh elimination by winning an overwhelming majority in the newly elected Majlis.

However, a small group of right-wing politicians, opposed to Qavam and his Democrats, also managed to get elected. Among them was Dr. Mohammed Mossadegh; he had served nearly thirty years in the Majlis and had become a formidable force. In succeeding years he was to become even more formidable. He put himself above any "party loyalty" and could well be described as a political megalomaniac. Winning the support of H.I.M., he nationalized the Anglo-Iranian Oil Company. Then he expelled the British from Iran. Growing in confidence, he allied himself with the revivified Tudeh and their Russian backers and turned on the Shah himself. By now he had not only made implacable enemies of the British; he had also alarmed President Eisenhower, who had just assumed office, and the new U.S. government—most especially John Foster Dulles, Secretary of State, and his brother Allen, Director of the CIA. Churchill, then Prime Minister of England, Anthony Eden,* Foreign Secretary, and other British elements combined their different concern. The result was AJAX.

But to return to 1946: The Shah had, in addition to grappling with Iran's tremendous foreign problems, begun to direct his country's attention toward the problems of modernization and Westernization of its internal structure. The government factories estab-

---

*See *Memoirs of Anthony Eden: Full Circle,* Houghton, 1960, Chapter 9 of Book One.

lished by Reza Shah were seriously run down, so a new organization, the Industrial and Mineral Bank, was set up to revivify and coordinate these activities. The Shah also wanted a national plan for economic development drawn up. To this end he appointed a committee to prepare a Seven Year Plan.

The draft produced by this committee proved to be extremely ambitious. Its program was far too expensive for the government's available resources. Iran therefore called for the support promised in the Tripartite Treaty, and the Western-created International Bank for Development and Reparations seemed a natural source of assistance. It agreed to study the program and sent American experts to do so in detail.

The fifteenth Majlis, the election of which had been delayed for six months by the struggle with Russia over the northern provinces, finally began sessions in the summer of 1947. Thus, two major problems—the Soviet demand for an oil concession and national economic development—came to a boil at the same moment.

One might more accurately say that *three* boilings were involved, all springing from but one kettle. First was the Soviet demand, which was not flatly rejected. While resolving that Qavam had acted in good faith in the agreement he had reached with the Soviets, the Majlis nonetheless pronounced the agreement of April 1946 that established a joint Russian-Iranian oil company to be null and void. However, it did conclude that if there proved to be commercial oil resources in the northern provinces, Iran would negotiate with the Soviet Union for their sale.

Second, in the bill's final paragraph, the Majlis turned its attention to the Anglo-Iranian Oil Company. The bill stated that the "government is bound in all cases where the rights of the Iranian nation have been damaged in connection with the national resources, whether underground or otherwise, particularly concerning the oil fields of the south, to make necessary negotiations and to take steps for demanding the settlement of these rights. . . ."*

Thirdly, while the American company employed by the International Bank had submitted its report, calling for expenditures far larger than Iran could afford, the report was implicitly, if not explicitly, clear that a bank in which the British were playing a major role would not help finance a move to dispossess a British company. The British as well as the Russians were being eliminated from the Iranian oil picture. The ultimate question was: From where could Iran obtain funds to keep going without oil revenue?

It was at this point—the summer of 1947—that my wife Polly and I went on what was to be the first of many joint visits. Among other writing projects, I had agreed to do a book, later called *Arabs, Oil and History,* which included a chapter on Iran. I remembered how we had driven in from Baghdad, crossing the frontier at Khanequin. Most vividly I recalled the drive beyond, through the mountains to Kermanshah. Stories of banditry in the hills and valleys between the border and Kermanshah made us quite nervous. I had a loaded pistol on the floor of the car between my feet, but it probably would have been of little help had we been ambushed. We spent the night in an old-fashioned *khaimakham* in Kermanshah before driving on the next morning through Hamadan to Teheran— the same route the colonel commanding at Kermanshah would later follow in August 1953 in his march to support the Shah.

*Text quoted in Shamim, Ali Asghar, *Iran in the Reign of His Majesty Mohammad Reza Shah Pahlavi,* Teheran, 1966, pp. 74–75.

So began a most varied and exciting visit. Of the greatest importance was my first audience with H.I.M. The Shah had received me at his palace at Saadabad. I was then all of thirty-one years old, the Shah not yet twenty-eight. He made a lasting impression on me, striking me as an intense young man, with a wiry body and a wiry spirit also—dark, slim, with a deep store of barely hidden energy. His personality was subdued at that time. This was due partly, no doubt, to advice he was getting from well-meaning individuals, including the American Ambassador, George Allen. Ignoring Iran's long history, which has always centered on the monarchy, everyone urged him to create immediately a Western-style democracy. Positive that this could not be done "immediately," the Shah was not yet certain of what he *should* do. Ambassadorial advice was obviously not the proper solution.

During our interview the Shah made the point that, while his training had been largely military, he was convinced that the most important front in Iran was the civilian front. He put it quite simply: "As long as the Iranian people are ill-fed, ill-clothed, ill-educated and just plain ill, there can be no real security against outside aggression. An army can be defeated, a people cannot. But the people must be strong, united, and convinced in their cause. Therefore," he continued, "the course Iran must follow is all too clear. The government *must* institute a program of free public education, free hospitals and clinics, and of economic improvements." Particularly important in his opinion were irrigation and agricultural methods which would provide Iranians with their basic necessities—food and clothing. His analysis was unquestionably sound. But how was he to get the government to take the action he saw to be necessary?

As one looks back on it, the Shah's situation in 1947

was then cloudy, uncertain, very difficult to evaluate. What *was* his real power? How did one estimate the strength of the opposition? More accurately, it was oppositions, plural, for there was no single, united force opposing him. Rather, it was a conglomerate of forces, often divided and hostile one to the other. The landed class was selfish for its own interests. The religious leaders, the mullahs, were too suspicious of any possible ally to enter meaningful relationships. The tribes, especially the Qashqai, were enemy to, and feared by, all parties. Considering what he was up against, the Shah's sense of inner confidence was surprising and most impressive. Then I had bid him farewell with mixed feelings of concern and confidence. The Qashqai were enemies, the religious leaders doubtful, but the landed class had on the whole joined with the army and the people in H.I.M.'s support.

Later, on that same visit, at H.I.M.'s instruction, the head of the National Bank discussed the seven-year program by which the government hoped to effect the major aims of the policy he had outlined to me. I found the man more impressive than his presentation. One of the most serious problems the Shah faced was the shortage of able bureaucrats. The banker talking to me was able enough himself, but single-handed he could not assemble all the data required for meaningful discussion. The conversation added more to my concern than to my confidence.

Trying to eliminate my personal attachments, I recalled that in 1947 I could see four essential elements in the Iranian political setup. These were, first and foremost, the young Shah himself; secondly, the army; thirdly, the civilian politicians; and fourthly, the tribes. The political dance was marked by frequent changes of partners, but no music had yet been written that was able to bring the army and the tribes together. Few tunes appealed to the taste of both the Shah and the civilian politicians, but H.I.M. had found that the army could follow his steps very well. No civilian politician, not even Qavam, was strong in himself. They were, however, a tightly knit federation and could put up quite a struggle against anyone trying to break their hold on the government. The Shah had enjoyed great popular support, particularly because of the firm manner in which he stood up to the Russians in the northwest a year earlier. The army, well under his control, gained strength from its alliance with him. It was the tribes that I found to be really alarming, bearing out what Bunche and Upton had earlier told me. They were vigorous, rich, well armed and determined. They had the most powerful single, cohesive bloc of representatives in the Majlis. This was a relatively small bloc (thirty-five out of 136), but if it retained its unity it could exert influence out of all proportion to its size. Strong central government was bound to limit the independence of the tribes, but the question was, where was strong central government to be found?

Thus I remembered most vividly my first encounter with the Qashqai. This was on a visit to Shiraz, in the south, as guest of the four principal Qashqai khans. The old Shah, Reza Pahlavi, had made determined efforts to crush the strength of the tribes, especially the Qashqai. He tried to get their rifles away, settle them in villages and entice their leaders to Teheran, where he held them hostage. To some extent and with some tribes, he succeeded in his aim. The Bakhtiari, for instance, were pretty well subdued. But when Reza Shah was deposed by the British and Russians in 1941, the tribes benefited from the presence of foreign armies and the confusion of a distant war to accumulate more rifles than they ever had before. The result was that, far from being a vanishing way of life, they regained much of the strength they had lost under Reza Shah. The Qashqai in particular were reputed to be fierce and effective warriors; they were certainly consummate politicians. For many years past they had hated the British. Of the Americans they were uncertain but hopeful. The Germans were out of things, at least for the moment. And the Russians were truly problematical. The alliance that would blossom during AJAX days was hard to foresee then.

We, my wife Polly and I, had been received in Shiraz by Khosro Khan, the youngest of the four brothers who were the rulers of the Qashqai. What became the Shah's palace in Shiraz was at that time the Qashqai mansion-headquarters. We sat with Khosro Khan in a lovely, restful, cool room with the sound of running water, which splashed from a fountain at the head of the room and ran, through a central tiled channel in the floor, out into the garden at the other end. The sight of green grass and tall cypress trees through windows on either side was soothing to eye and spirit. We had just finished one of the roughest, and certainly by any standard the hottest, airplane trips we had ever made.

Now, when the heat of the day had broken, we could walk in the garden, admire what is reputed to be the tallest cypress tree in the world and inspect the roses, zinnias and sweet william that grew in profusion beside numerous tiled pools. We could look on the colorful mosaics and carvings which decorated the outer walls of the palace. The sculpted lions, walking like proud kings, would remind us of our ancient history books which pictured the reigns of Cyrus the Great and Darius thousands of years earlier. We were only a few miles from the ruins of their imperial capital, Persepolis, still one of the most impressive and beautiful sights in the world. Its pillars stand straight and mighty above the sand; its bas-reliefs show emperors locked in mortal combat with lions or with queer one-horned beasts. I thought then that perhaps these imaginary animals might be the fabled unicorn. I suspect now that they are oryx and that they really have two parallel horns, looking—in bas-relief—like one. Other sculptures show the emperors receiving tribute of conquered kings from Greece, from Ethiopia to as far away as Cathay. I have been back to Persepolis many times since this first visit, and it never ceases to impress and amaze me. The 2,500th anniversary of Persian monarchy celebration was held there in 1971, an awesome, magnificent occasion.

Shiraz has long been known for pleasant life, fine silver, wine, roses and wit. Our host seemed entirely at home. Khosro Khan was a stocky, smiling young man, wearing a double-breasted blue suit, who looked somewhat like an American college boy, a football player. He offered us ice-cold beer and, smiling broadly, asked, "Is this a good introduction to nomadic tribal life? Would you think this was the headquarters of the Qashqai?"

The answer was clearly "No."

When we think of nomads, we think of black wool tents, of humped camels stretched along a desert sky in stark silhouette, flocks of goats and sheep ever moving in the constant search for grass. We think also, even more now than we did then, of a way of life that is close to vanishing, just as the red Indians and the buffalo have practically vanished from our own country. That picture was not at that time entirely correct. But the number of nomads was constantly decreasing. More and more of them were being forcibly settled on the land or given steady employment—for instance, in the great oil fields of Iraq, Saudi Arabia and Iran itself. The government was making a steady effort to absorb the tribes into stable, national life. Improved agricultural methods and ambitious irrigation projects were being advanced, so that lands whose sparse yield had barely supported a few families can now feed hundreds, even thousands of inhabitants. But the nomads, notably the Qashqais, were not then being easily absorbed.

Khosro Khan made that very clear. First he told of a very neat trick his brothers, Mohammed Hosayn Khan and Malik Mansour Khan, had played on the Nazis during the war. In 1939 the two of them had been studying in Berlin. A Persian, working for the Nazis, approached Malik Mansour and urged him to support a movement in Iran against Reza Shah. Malik Mansour wanted to get home. He pretended to be eager to help and proposed to enlist the support of his oldest brother, Nasser Khan. He convinced the Abwehr that Nasser Khan, if supplied with money and arms, could provide the Axis with most effective aid. Therefore the Abwehr organized a secret mission, consisting of five Germans and a Persian liaison officer named Fahd. The latter had been hand-picked by Malik Mansour and carried—in addition to the official messages given the group—secret and quite contrary messages to Nasser Khan. The mission also took, in addition to arms and explosives, $100,000 in U.S. bills.

Dropped by parachute into southern Iran, they landed some distance from their destination. However, they managed to reach the Qashqai tribe. Here, except for Fahd, they received an unpleasant surprise. Nasser Khan confiscated all their weapons and equipment, including the $100,000. Then, well satisfied, he informed the British consul in Shiraz of their capture, saying that he would hold them as guarantee for the safety of his brothers. Meanwhile, Malik Mansour had persuaded the Germans to allow him to go to Istanbul to serve as a forward base. From thence he was able to make his way to Teheran.

The German agents, with the exception of their leader—who committed suicide in order to avoid capture—were later turned over to the British. Everyone except the Germans had made a good profit on the deal.

In October 1946 there was fighting between the tribes and the Iranian Army. The Qashqai had captured some 2,000 rifles as well as light artillery and tanks. Since the tribes lacked training in "tanksmanship" or use of artillery, Khosro Khan disdainfully returned all but the rifles to Teheran. My friend Alex Gagarine, then assistant U.S. military attaché in Teheran, was instructed to survey the scene of the fighting and report to Washington. The Iranian Army and the Qashqai, both anxious to make good impressions, gave him passes. In a jeep with a U.S. flag implanted on it he took off for the front. The army let him through without difficulty, but in the no man's zone men of a tribe allied with the Qashqai fired on him and pursued his jeep. Alex fired back, killing one horse and discouraging pursuit. Thereupon Reuters reported that American forces had "wiped out close to a score of tribesmen in a pitched battle."

Later this discourteous behavior to his American friends was reported to Khosro Khan, who, it was said, expressed his displeasure by riding over to the village of the offending tribe and shooting their head man dead. When I asked him if this were true, he smiled and shrugged his shoulders. He made no other reply.

We were returned to Teheran courtesy of the Qashqais, accompanied by the local "stringer" for the

Associated Press, a young, bespectacled Iranian journalist. Our auto trip allowed for a stop in Isfahan, the first visit for Polly, and much instructive talk with the journalist. We were appreciably better educated when we reached the capital. There Alex Gagarine introduced us to a strapping youth who, in later years, I thought to have been Ardeshir Zahedi. In fact Ardeshir did not come back from the United States, where he attended college in Salt Lake City, until somewhat later. At that time he worked under Bill Warne, head of the technical assistance program (Point Four, as it was known) in Teheran. The young man to whom Alex actually introduced us was, I now find, named Jehanjir Khan; I have never seen him since.

Polly and I then made a trip up to the Caspian coast before leaving Iran, but essentially our visit was over. As we left the country, my thoughts reverted to the talk with the National Bank head and to another conversation, this with a young critic of the administration. He was impatient with "plans." There had been too many of them. How, he asked, was action to be obtained? He answered his own question by saying "only by cleaning out the present government and the governing class, root and branch." I wondered how that could be done. The young man gave me a simple answer. "First," he said, "you might buy out the present ruling clique of a thousand. But where could you get the money to do this? Secondly, you might make an example of five or fifteen or an appropriate number of the ruling clique by trying them for crimes and hanging them. This," he thought, "would scare off the others, but who in the present government would have the determination to do it?" That was the third question and left only one answer, which was, in his mind, revolution.

To my mind, however, it also left a fourth most

important question: Revolution by whom? I could see no group in Iran which combined the incentive, strength, program and persistence to make a successful revolution without foreign, presumably Russian, support.

But all who did reach that evaluation were overlooking the most important figure in the country. It was the Shah, H.I.M. the Shahanshah Aryamehr himself, who was to create and lead the revolution. He made it a most successful one.

CHAPTER

4

"For he who shuffles is not he who cuts, and one performance is worth two promises."

Miguel de Cervantes Saavedra (d. 1616)

My train of thought about the past was interrupted by arrival in Paris. I had to spend the night in a hotel near the airport and change airlines—from Pan American to Air France— so that I could get a more direct flight to Beirut. Once I was in the sky again early the next morning, I resumed my recollections. The time period I was reviewing involved bloodshed and attempted assassination. It would end with the establishment of relations with the men who were to be the principal agents of AJAX. Back in 1950 I did not recognize them as "harbingers of spring," and I could hardly foresee their participation in an undertaking that we had not yet conceived. Not surprisingly, they were well ahead of us on that score; they had the gift and the foresight to spot what *must* happen. Deliberately, I now remember only their pseudonyms; they were the Boscoe brothers.

Confronted by a parliamentary crisis and unable to reunite his divided Democratic Party, Qavam ended his long rule as Prime Minister when in December 1947 he submitted his resignation. The Shah, with recollections of Azerbaijan and the old man's visit to Moscow still fresh in his mind, was happy to accept it. There followed a series of Prime Ministers, most of whose names entirely slip my mind. Meanwhile, H.I.M. himself was concentrating on economic development. The Majlis had approved his Seven Year Plan, which approval was followed almost immediately by creation of the Plan Organization to carry out the national intent. This was the first of the Shah's serious, continuing efforts of measures for rapid industrialization of Iran. Included among its objectives were improved transportation and communications, electric power, irrigation, public health, education and the organization of new industries. Most important was to be large-scale exploitation of Iran's mineral resources. I smiled wryly at the memory, for the Plan never really got off the ground. It needed financial backing from abroad and could not get it. In a couple of years it was suspended. Perhaps if AJAX were successful it could be started up again.

Meanwhile the Russians, because of their defeat in Azerbaijan, had abandoned their hopes for an oil concession. They were still willing to bide their time. But only for the time being. During that "time being" the Shah set to work to solidify his control over the basic political and economic resources of his country. The armed forces were solidly his. However, the people at large were not yet truly an effective ally. Loyal they were and proud of their heritage. But they did not share a common understanding of that heritage. The majority of them were illiterate and, worse, they were illiterate in different languages. Thus education, especially in the reading and writing of Persian (or Farsi, its traditional name) had to be the first, basic requirement of building a new country.

The second essential, the primary economic resource, was oil. Anyone could clearly see that there was a lot of it and that it promised to be a tremendous source of wealth. Unfortunately, it was not in Iranian hands. The oil fields had been drilled, produced and owned by a British company, which operated in British, not Iranian, interests. This was something the Shah had to face—and to change.

Thus, in the spring of 1948, negotiations between Iran and the Anglo-Iranian Oil Company had begun on a serious basis. A British director, N. A. Gass, arrived in Teheran announcing the unwillingness of the company to consider any extensive revision of the 1933 agreement. The company was ready to deal with whatever violations of that agreement, if any, the Iranians could prove. The Iranian negotiator, Hakimi, was inadequately prepared, Gass supremely stubborn. The talks failed; the Shah and Mossadegh, quite separately but for the same reasons, were both angry, and on June 8, 1948, Hakimi resigned. His successors did little better. Gass again came to Teheran, but while his position had hardly changed, there were new forces emerging in Iran that discarded the moderate approach of the constitutionalists in favor of violence and terror. "Their appearance," observes Ramesh Sanghvi, "ushered in an era where the assassin's gun was used more often than the ballot box."*

This violence had been directed, often irrationally,

*Anyamehr: The Shah of Iran, London: Transorient, 1968, p. 159.

in many directions. The Shah, as the leader most obviously growing in stature and acceptability, came under the special attack of extremist groups—the Fadayun-I-Islam, a small party led by the fanatic Sa'ed Nawab Safavi, and the Mujahidin-Islam, first under Shams Qanatabadi, an opportunist of no real significance, but later taken over by the Ayatollah Mullah Mustapha Kashani, a far more redoubtable figure. The two groups lived on support from the mullahs, the Moslem "clerical" class, and religious students, both of whom had followers among the more superstitious elements of urban workers. The Shah's active intervention for improving education and technology, for modernizing the country, aroused their hatred and frustration. Later, as the Communist Tudeh gained more power through their influence on Mossadegh, these "religious" elements were greatly weakened in their position. No longer were they *the* leaders of opposition to the Shah. They became in effect a third party, uncommitted to either side. Now, in 1953, we were making an effort to win their support. They hedged, tried to bargain. We certainly did want help wherever we could find it. But I did not believe them worth the time, trouble and, most important apparently to them, the money that would be required. So we decided to go ahead without them, and they lost the opportunity—which was not to come again—to give H.I.M. some reason to feel obligated to them. In any case, he would have found it difficult to forget that in 1949 and 1950 their animosity, and their ammunition, was directed against him.

The hatred of the mullahs had been dramatically headlined by near disaster. On February 4, 1949, the Shah attended a ceremony at Teheran University. He was to address the students on the day of annual celebrations and was wearing—as he did on most formal occasions—his military uniform. He remembers the events vividly, and he has told me of them several times.

"I got out of my car expecting nothing, thinking only of what I was to say. What I noted first was a bang—a shot. Then quickly more shots. The first three struck my cap. I was in uniform, with a visored cap and a top projecting over the visor. These shots went through without, by some miracle, hitting me. The fourth, also miraculously, went through my cheek and upper lip. It came out under my nose. I don't know why.

"By now I had spotted the man who was trying to kill me. He was only two yards away, aiming his revolver straight at my heart. What was I to do?"

I must say that throughout his life the Shah's courage, and his sense of destiny, have been remarkable.

As he put it: "Both the would-be assassin and I were now clear of any crowd, which had naturally scattered at the shots. He had a clear field of fire. At such point-blank range, how could he miss again?

"What could I do? Jump on him? But the closer I got, the better target I'd be. Should I run away? Then he'd hit me in the back. So I started evasive movements— you could call it shadow-dancing or feinting. He fired again, wounding me in the shoulder. Then, thanks be to God, his gun jammed. The last shot would not go off. I had the queer, but certainly not unpleasant, sensation of knowing that I had lived through it!

"I even remember clearly what happened after. Naturally, the man tried to escape. He threw down his useless gun and started to run. Unfortunately some of my young officers shot too well, and they killed him. To interrogate him could have been valuable.

"He must have been a curious character. We found he'd been friendly with various religious fanatics, arch-conservatives, of course. But his small flat—

if you can call it that—also had literature of the Tudeh Communist Party. And strangely, his mistress was the daughter of a gardener at the British Embassy! I attach no significance to that," he added, smiling.

"Of course I was bleeding like a young bull whose throat had been cut." (In America we'd say "like a stuck pig," but Moslems regard pigs as dirty unmentionables.) "My own wish was to go ahead with the speech. However, my entourage overruled me. Instead they took me to the hospital. There I was able, and *allowed*—" he grinned again— "to make a radio report to my people saying that by the grace of God I was still alive. The assassination attempt had failed."

Our Ambassador to Iran, John Wiley, was home on consultation at the time. The *chargé d'affaires* cabled Washington that the would-be assassin was alleged to be a member of a fanatical Moslem society, Parcham-I-Islam— "Flag of Islam." This is a society I have been unable to identify, but there was a newspaper of that name from which the attacker, whose name was Nasser Fakhrara'i, carried a press card. Iranian friends have told me that some evidence pointed to an association with Fadayun-I-Islam. There was other evidence suggesting Tudeh connections, as the Shah had mentioned.

The Shah, I recalled, had also told me of earlier intimations of divine protection. As a child he had been riding horseback, held on the saddle pommel by a servant behind him. They were going down a steep, stony slope when the horse stumbled. The young crown prince had been flung over the mount's head straight onto sharp rocks below. "Divine forces" held him up; otherwise his head would have been crushed. On another occasion, he was suffering from a severe, inexplicable fever. The Imam Ali, revered by predominantly Shiite* Iran, appeared to him in a dream, giving him a bowl of gruel. Mohammed Reza Pahlavi drank it, and when he awakened the fever had gone.

Another dramatic occasion had been not long after the attempted assassination outside the university. In the spring of 1949 he had flown south of Teheran to inspect the site of an irrigation dam near Isfahan. On the return journey he took off, as usual piloting the plane himself, with the military commander of the area as his only companion in a single-engine aircraft. Some ten minutes after takeoff, when they were too far from the field to make it safely back, the engine went dead. There was no alternative but to make a forced landing in the mountainous terrain below. Although such a catastrophe would seem to bring certain death, H.I.M. landed the plane safely and skillfully. In his autobiography he recorded the incident in these sober words:

> As every pilot knows, a plane has a stalling speed below which it will go into a spin. With the engine gone, I had no throttle, nor could I maneuver within the narrow confines of the ra/ine; the only thing was to maintain speed by going down then and there. Just before we struck, I pulled on the stick to raise the plane's nose to avert a head-on collision with the barrier of rock lying directly in front of us. The plane had barely enough speed left to clear the barrier and could not surmount a boulder lying just beyond. When we collided with it, the undercarriage was completely torn off, but at least that helped to reduce our speed. The plane started to slide on its belly over the rock-strewn ground. A moment later, the propeller hit a large boulder, which made it turn a slow and deliberate somersault, coming to a halt with the fuselage upside down. Neither of us had suffered so much as a scratch. . . . Was that narrow escape good luck, or was it good luck bolstered by something else?*

One result of the assassination attempt on the Shah's life in February was the countrywide realization that his disappearance would result in total anarchy. The government responded by outlawing the Tudeh and ordering the arrest of leaders of the right-wing fanatics, including the Ayatollah Kashani. Even Qavam, though the Shah intervened on his behalf, was obliged to flee the country. The Majlis activated constitutional provisions authorizing a Senate, half the members to be elected, half appointed by the Shah. (Until then the Majlis had been a one-house parliamentary body.) It also determined that basic changes in the Constitution were required, and a Constituent Assembly was therefore convened. On May 8, 1949, this formally gave the Shah power to dissolve either or both houses of the Majlis; it provided as well for amendments to the Constitution, excluding, however, those articles concerning Islam and the authority of the monarchy.

At this point the Shah, in the hope of obtaining support to activate the Seven Year Plan, had resolved to visit the United States. On his state visit of November 1949 the Achesons (Dean then being Secretary of State) gave what Dean described as "one of the gayer state dinners for H.I.M. at Anderson House."** In the official talks H.I.M. explained the main features of his program, including the requisitioning from landlords of extensive tracts of farm land. The redistribution of the land was to be accomplished by governmental sale of tracts to farmers on terms that would allow them to pay back the government in twenty to twenty-five years. This particular project had to be postponed because, as he put it, he received a friendly reception

*Mission for My Country, p. 56.
**Acheson, op. cit., p. 502.

in the States but returned "completely empty-handed."* There were, he recognized, still major psychological consequences in Congress from the collapse of the Kuomintang (Chiang Kai-shek) regime in China, to which Congress tended to compare the Shah's regime. Iran did not present a convincing picture of stability or even of firm leadership. Upon returning to Iran, he conducted a vigorous campaign for governmental reform and efficiency. Corrupt officials were dismissed and an anticorruption campaign was begun. Plans for basic land reform were prepared, but the only step taken at the time was the distribution of crown lands, which H.I.M. decreed in early 1950.

He was bitterly disappointed by the way Washington perceived Iran. As partial compensation for the rebuff, he accepted a Soviet trade agreement of $20 million to show the West that he could, if and when he wished, turn to their enemy (and his also) for help. Washington did try again. In the spring of 1950 Henry Grady, who had been a most successful Ambassador to Greece, was transferred to Iran. The U.S. Embassy there was strengthened by assignment of a competent economic mission and began pressing the State Department for a major aid program. But as Acheson has reported:

> We failed again; for a year the State Department and the field fumbled the financial ball between them. We lacked decisiveness and vigor; they suffered from the habit learned in Athens of thinking in terms of large financial resources, with the result that both the mission and the Shah disdained the funds available, nothing got done, and confidence suffered all around. By the autumn of 1950 tempers became badly frayed.**

Proposed loans by the World Bank and the U.S.

*Mission for My Country, p. 88.
**Acheson, op. cit., p. 502.

Export-Import Bank were rejected, both by the Iranian government and the U.S. Embassy, as insultingly small. Grady called for a loan of $100 million for its psychological effect, but the State Department had no funds and the lending agencies felt that Iran, in the absence of an oil agreement, "did not look like a good risk."*

Meanwhile, negotiations with Gass and the Anglo-Iranian Oil Company had continued through the first half of the year. In July 1950 Gass and Finance Minister Golshayan signed an agreement which did increase royalties from four to six shillings per ton—plus an immediate payment of 23 million pounds to cover credits already accrued. But the news of the formula leaked, and it met immediate opposition from the public and the Majlis. Mossadegh and the Tudeh led the outcry. No vote had been tallied when the term of the fifteenth Majlis ended on August 7, and preparations for the new election began in a state of turmoil. The battle area for the next three years had been marked out.

The Shah and Mossadegh politically were drawing closer. They shared one objective—Iran's determination to get just compensation for its oil—but they differed substantially on everything else. The Shah had grown in realism, leadership and planning ability. Mossadegh was like an ill-tempered, erratic old peasant, continuing on the fringe of responsibility and reality but still judging all problems from his emotional standpoint. His day of power was rapidly approaching.

The new Majlis assembled in February 1950, and Prime Minister Sa'ed, aware that the Majlis, the

*Ibid.

people and the Shah all opposed the Golshayan–Gass agreement, did not defend it seriously. On March 22 he resigned, and Ali Mansur was named to take his place. Agitators in the streets were already calling for "nationalization now." Ali Mansur did not agree. He was voted out of office in June and replaced by General Haj Ali Razmarah. Razmarah tried to distract the Majlis by proposals for strengthening local self-government, but it would not be distracted. In November it resolved that the government's statements on oil should not be confirmed. On the contrary, they were totally rejected. This brought about renewed agitation against foreigners and condemnation of Razmarah. Mossadegh then demanded nationalization of the entire Iranian oil industry.

By this time, because of the Korean war, I had been called back to work in the Central Intelligence Agency. Meanwhile, the Boscoe brothers, my "harbingers of spring," had made their approach. The target they selected was Roger Black, one of the two OSS hands I had met in early 1944.

Roger was a crusty, quixotic, opinionated professor who spoke fluent Farsi. It was natural for him to be suspected of being an Agency man. He knew far more of Iran and of the people than any of us actually in the Agency did—or probably ever would. But he was a character with an unpredictable mind of his own; he would run things his own way whatever the rest of us might think. So we did think—and decided that Roger was far more than we could handle. We maintained friendly contact. He brought us, without solicitation, all sorts of fascinating but generally irrelevant bits of information: on *khaimakhans*, teahouses, between the religious center Qum and Isfahan; on bearded types, who reminded me of Mahboub Ali in Kipling's *Kim* and who roamed the mountains and deserts of eastern Iran; and on scholarly, often revolutionary, intrigues that flourished in the college faculties among whom he lived. We did not take all his information seriously, though we found it interesting, often entertaining. It struck me as odd, at first, that the Boscoe brothers had thought Professor Black to be with the CIA, but later I decided that they were simply sure that he *must* have CIA contacts.

We were also very lucky that Roger, without examining them too closely, simply passed them along to my senior representative. Roger was, for reasons that were never clear to me, a strong supporter of Dr. Mossadegh. Perhaps he found the crotchety old man a *sympatico* type, not unlike himself in many of his—to me—less important characteristics. They were, after all, both vain, opinionated, domineering. If that is all Mossadegh had been, he wouldn't have worried me either. Or the Boscoes.

As it was, George Cuvier found the two brothers far more interesting than did Roger. This was late in 1950, and I was due shortly in Iran on one of my frequent visits. He introduced them to me in one of our "safe houses"* on the outskirts of the city. The brothers were quiet, businesslike, very impressive men, one a large, solidly built, dark chap who was a lawyer, the other also dark but shorter, slim, apparently younger (in his late twenties, I guessed) and more talkative, a journalist by profession. There was, for that part of the world where directness is not a local characteristic, no beating about the bush. They came right to the point. Mossadegh was not yet in power but they thought it only a matter of time, a short time, before he would be. They foresaw a dangerous alliance between him, perhaps the rebellious mullahs, certainly the Tudeh, and behind them the Russians. They did not like what

---

*Houses occupied by non-Agency Americans or Iranians, used for clandestine meeting places.

they foresaw (neither did I), and they wanted American help to work in support of the Shah. My prophetic abilities were not up to theirs. I was further concerned because, although it was clear that they had had some sort of clandestine training, they would not tell me from whom.

They also claimed to have an organization to support them but would not identify its members. Nonetheless, I was so impressed that I arranged to finance their travel to the U.S., where we could test and evaluate their capabilities more thoroughly. One would come via Germany, where he had business interests which would excuse his absence from Iran; the other (the reporter) would travel by way of France, where he could occupy himself on behalf of his newspaper. They could meet me in Washington within two months. By then the outlook on Dr. Mossadegh might have become more clear.

Once they arrived in the United States, we got down to the serious business of interrogation, verification, and establishing their qualifications to do the job they were promising to do. We gave them the whole works, including thorough tests of their veracity. To the questions on their former association and their present subordinate supporters, they would not, as they had told us, answer. Carefully we explained that while we, knowing them, might be sure of their veracity and their value, we had superiors who were bound to be skeptical—if only because they were more remote. How, without knowing more of their background and the nature of their present strength, could we persuade the Director of Central Intelligence of their true worth? They smiled and shrugged their shoulders. That was our problem, they said, up to us to solve.

So we did. I went to Allen Dulles, and with him to Beedle Smith, and told my story. I described how these men had come to us, explaining why they had approached Roger Black, of whom naturally neither Allen nor Beedle had ever heard; why Cuvier and I had been impressed by them; and finally why, in spite of their refusal to tell us all we wanted to know, I still had confidence in their ability to do what they promised they would. After all, we had carefully verified their loyalty to the Shah and their hatred of Mossadegh.

In any case, after considerable discussion and soul-searching, Allen and Beedle gave me the green light to enlist them as working allies in support of the Shah. I returned to the Boscoes stating that they had been given provisional clearance, that we would seek some early occasion to test their qualifications, and the strength of their organization, in action. That came sooner than we had expected.

CHAPTER
5

"The stars have us to bed;
Night draws the curtains, which the sun withdraws;
Music and light attend our head."

George Herbert (d. 1633)

My plane landed at Rome's Fiumicino Airport, and I had more than an hour on the ground before taking off for Beirut. I wandered around the building, had a couple of Campari and sodas and continued my musing over the past.

By now I had reviewed events up to the days of Prime Minister General Ali Razmarah. Like so many other Persians before the "new" Shah had made his authority felt, Razmarah had been an opportunist, without discernible convictions. Until the fall of 1946 he was, or pretended to be, pro-Tudeh. He was close to

Mozaffar Firuz, then a minister in Qavam's cabinet, and later Ambassador to Russia. Firuz was strongly pro-Tudeh. But Razmarah came to realize that power was in the hands of the Shah. By the time of H.I.M.'s move against Azerbaijan in December 1946, he had committed himself to the royal camp and there he remained, although his loyalty was still questioned by some. It was no longer open to question after the spring of 1951. He had become Prime Minister in June 1950. When Mossadegh demanded nationalization of the entire oil industry, Razmarah made what proved to be his fatal commitment.

He had appealed to the AIOC to sweeten the Supplemental Oil Agreement, which had been initialed by both parties in July 1949. (A year later the Oil Commission of the Majlis had recommended its rejection.) What Razmarah wanted was concessions on points the Majlis had criticized which would cost the British nothing. He asked that Iran have the right to inspect the books of the company—after all, Iran was a 20 percent owner; that Iranian personnel in the company be increased; that oil sold in Iran be priced on cost, not on world prices; and that Iran be informed of where its oil was being sold. U. S. Assistant Secretary of State George McGhee appealed to the British Foreign Office and AIOC to grant these requests, which were truly insubstantial. But neither would budge one inch. In January 1951, just as the Majlis was directing its Oil Commission to recommend new legislation—which meant nationalization—the Arabian-American Oil Company (Aramco) announced a new contract that assured Saudi Arabia of 50 percent profits. At the end of February, AIOC did finally express readiness to reopen negotiations along the Aramco terms. For some reason Razmarah kept this offer to himself. He stuck to the argument that, in the face of Iranian incompetence to produce and market its oil, Iran must reach a settlement with the British.*

On March 3 the Prime Minister told the Majlis that nationalization would be impracticable as well as illegal. This produced the predictable uproar. There was a movement in the army against him. Imprisoned Tudeh leaders escaped with the help of army officers, and the Fedayun denounced Razmarah as an irreligious madman. On March 7, while attending the funeral of a mullah, he was assassinated by a Fedayun fanatic. On the 19th, his Minister of Education, Azam Zanganeh, was also shot and died a few days later. Before Razmarah's successor, Hussein Ala, could win the required vote of confidence in the Majlis, its oil committee did recommend nationalization. This was confirmed by the whole Majlis on the 15th. The Shah was concerned that Iran lacked the knowledge and experience to operate the huge oil enterprise in its south. More importantly, he was convinced that national humiliation could no longer be endured. He endorsed the nationalization and expropriation law, which was approved by the Majlis on April 19. As Dean Acheson observed, referring to AIOC, "Never had so few lost so much so stupidly and so fast."**

Meanwhile, Ala, still favoring a compromise proposal, had met with Sir Francis Shepherd, the British Ambassador, who totally rejected the measure. Following this, Ala announced to the cabinet his inability to continue and submitted his resignation to the Shah. Seven governments had fallen between 1946 and 1951; a dramatic move was necessary. Much as H.I.M. might distrust Mossadegh, the old man was gaining ever more popular backing. A "popular" Pre-

*Acheson, *op. cit.*, pp. 503 *et seq.*
**Ibid.*, p. 504.

mier had become a practical necessity. Mossadegh had promised much to the people. "In fact," as H.I.M. was to write later, "how could anyone be against Mossadegh? He would enrich everybody, he would fight the foreigner, he would secure our rights. No wonder students, intellectuals, people from all walks of life, flocked to his banner."

So now Mossadegh was summoned to the palace. The Shah promised support if he would carry out nationalization and raise the standard of living. Mossadegh accepted and became Prime Minister on the day that nationalization was approved. Nine days later the Majlis voted confidence in his government by the impressive majority of 99 to 3. This was, the Shah observed, "Mossadegh's greatest opportunity. His success had exceeded his own fondest dreams, as well as those of his followers. He was to enjoy my full support for a year and my toleration—agonizing though it was for me—during many months thereafter. What would he do?"*

The new Prime Minister gave his birth date as 1871 or 1881, depending whether he wanted to be just old or truly ancient. The date of 1881 is the correct one, which made him just seventy when he took office. Born into one of the rich land-owning families, he was educated in France and Switzerland. The struggle over Persia at that time was between Britain and Czarist Russia. Young Mossadegh opted for the former. With British backing he was elected to the Majlis in 1915. In due course he became governor, first of the province of Fars, later of Azerbaijan. His great strength lay in his ability to mesmerize crowds by his speechmaking. He could turn an audience into a prayer session or a raging monster. His wild exaggerations found ready acceptance, and frequently his own

*Mission for My Country, p. 91.

example led his listeners into almost insane hysteria. There was every indication, every promise, that as chief minister he would give the Shah the roughest, toughest ordeal—and possibly the best *oil* deal—that could be imagined. He had long since turned against the British; alliance with the Russians was yet to come. The United States he regarded as a useful tool to use against both. In the next two years all this would become painfully clear.

Mossadegh continued to hope that the Labour government in London would not support AIOC, but this hope was shaken ten days after his appointment. At that time Foreign Secretary Morrison protested the manner in which nationalization was being handled in southern Iran. Earlier, in the last days of March 1951, just before Mossadegh had taken office, a delegation led by Basil Jackson reached Teheran, but the talks made no progress. Morrison's protest was affected more by that than by the appointment of the new Prime Minister.

At April's end Mossadegh was installed. In early May, the body of Reza Shah was finally returned to Iran. It had been temporarily interred in South Africa after his death in 1943. Finally, arrangements had been completed to end the dead Shah's exile, which had been the result of Russian *and* British hostility. Now, in Iranian eyes, the British were the people chiefly responsible. They had become the target of all the accumulated resentments. The scene of Reza Shah's posthumous return is described by Leonard Mosley:*

Suddenly among the corps of marching members of the *majlis* . . . there shuffled by a tall, thin, bent old man with a haggard yellow face and a dripping nose,* which he did

*Mosley, *Power Play,* Baltimore: Penguin Books, 1974, pp. 198–99, 204.

not bother to wipe. [Cheering crowds] were hailing the leader of a newly formed coalition party, the National Front . . . [the announced purpose of which was] to wrest control of Iran's petroleum resources from the British. . . .

Soon both sides were striking attitudes which one might have thought had gone out of fashion with the death of Queen Victoria. For the British, the wogs were on the rampage. For the Iranians, a war of liberation had begun against the colonialists. What started out as reasonable discussion soon deteriorated into vituperation, threats, and violence.

In mid-June, Mossadegh had become totally disillusioned by British negotiating tactics. He announced the formation of the National Iranian Oil Company, NIOC. At the end of June a British cruiser was anchored off Abadan, sent to "protect the lives of British citizens," according to London. Its presence led tankers of flags other than British to leave Abadan without loading cargo. Meanwhile, the U.S. was growing alarmed, and President Truman himself felt a need for action. On July 5 he tried to be helpful, making a proposal for reconciliation and offering the services of Averell Harriman as a peacemaker.

Truman's alarm had been shared by others in Washington, especially by Secretary of State Dean Acheson and his close associates in the Department. Dean himself was first and foremost a friend of Great Britain. He had decided during World War II, when he was Assistant Secretary for Economic Affairs (and had persuaded "Wild Bill" Donovan to assign me to the Middle East on his behalf), that the British should have the primary role in the Middle East. Here, however,

*George McGhee, at that time Assistant Secretary of State for Near East and Africa, was quoted to me as remarking, at the time of Mossadegh's visit to the U.S. in 1952, "Mossadegh has a nose that makes Jimmy Durante look like an amputee!"

he did consider that they were overreacting to Dr. Mossadegh. On May 17, 1951, he had warned British Ambassador Sir Oliver Franks that the U.S. and the U.K. were seeing possible use of force in Iran quite differently.

The thought of Dean diverted me to even earlier memories. He was, I realized, far more patient in the foreign field, where his instinct was to avoid or at least postpone confrontation, then he was at home. His appearances before House or Senate committees brought out the combative side of his nature. In 1942 I attended a couple of sessions of the House Foreign Affairs Committee as his assistant. His mustachios bristling, his blue eyes frosty and his voice astringently acid, he dealt with questioners in a manner ranging from mild contempt, when he meant to be comparatively friendly, to cold arrogance when he thought—as he often did—the questions stupid. Congressman (later Senator) William Fulbright of Arkansas, who was in fact anything but stupid, was stubborn. He wanted his queries answered. Dean thought his desire for facts somewhat juvenile, and his voice dripped icicles as he responded.

But Oliver Franks was a good friend of his, and I am sure that although he was expressing profound misgivings about British intentions, he expressed them in a friendly way, giving the Ambassador benefit of any possible doubt. In his long account of his State Department experiences, *Present at the Creation,* Acheson summarized what he said to Franks:

> Only on invitation of the Iranian government, or Soviet military intervention, or a communist *coup d'état* in Teheran, or to evacuate British nationals in danger of attack, could we support the use of military force.[*]

[*]Acheson, *op. cit.*, p. 506. Acheson did not admit, even in the summer of 1953, the danger of "a Communist *coup d'état*."

He and Sir Oliver discussed the situation candidly, Sir Oliver reported to London, and the reply he received showed the difference of opinion to be deep indeed. At that point Acheson's final proposal, a last-ditch effort to stop, as he saw it, the drift to disaster, was that Averell Harriman be sent to Teheran in hope that he could re-establish a "negotiating pattern."

President Truman had accepted the proposal with enthusiasm. But Harriman was not exactly overjoyed by the prospect. The President immediately cabled Prime Minister Mossadegh, suggesting Harriman not as a mediator himself but as an emissary to promote the resumption of direct talks, in the interests of world peace, between Iranians and British. The first reaction from Teheran was cool, and London, already alerted to the possibility by Oliver Franks' cable of inquiry, was equally dubious. But further thought led both parties to welcome—or at least agree to—the offer. Truman held a formal farewell reception for Harriman where toasts were drunk to the success of the mission. The President, the former Secretary of State, at that time Secretary of Defense, General George Marshall and Dean Acheson were photographed wishing Harriman well. Reluctant or not, he was on his way.

In Teheran, meanwhile, the U.S.S.R. had been concentrating its efforts on rebuilding the Tudeh Party into a major political force. Considerable progress had been made. There was now not only a disciplined hard core but a substantial, if far less disciplined assortment, almost a mob, of Tudeh "members," mostly in Teheran but with significant elements in lesser cities, especially Kermanshah and Hamadan. From the south they had been in effect banned. The southwest, around Abadan, had a large Arab population which was politically passive; the central south—the heart of the old Persian empire—was under Qashqai domination; and the southeast was too far away, geographically, ethnically and politically, to offer the Tudeh promising opportunities for recruitment. The north likewise—from Azerbaijan east to Meshed—was, in the first place, anti-Russian; in the second, because of tribal and other local sentiments, it was unresponsive to Communist appeals. The country as a whole, with rare exceptions, was quite content to be anti-British. To be pro-Russian was another question.

Harriman had arrived on his mission to Teheran on July 15, 1951. He expected to be welcomed as a friend. "Instead what he got was a flea in his ear."*

> The Iranian Communist party, Tudeh, which was controlled and financed from Moscow, had now thrown its weight and money behind Mossadegh, and provided him with a street army of well-trained thugs. . . . Harriman, all prepared to smile and wave in acknowledgment to the cheering crowd he expected to meet on his way in from the airport, instead ran into an ugly demonstration from a column of Tudeh demonstrators armed with sticks and screaming anti-American slogans.**

Acheson reports*** that "several hundred" people were killed and twenty injured at his arrival. This seems a curious proportion of killed to injured and is as great an exaggeration as most other estimates of Iranian casualties during this period.

Meanwhile, Harriman had become thoroughly disillusioned. He and his interpreter, Colonel Vernon Walters (later the Deputy Director of the CIA), reported to Washington on their final meeting with Mossadegh: "Same record, played over on both sides!"

*Mosley, *op. cit.*, p. 207.
**_Ibid._, p. 208.
***Acheson, *op. cit.*, p. 508.

Harriman's mission had not turned out as President Truman and Secretary of State Acheson had anticipated. On the contrary, as Allen Dulles and I saw it, events were moving rapidly, inexorably toward conflict—between Mossadegh and the Shah and, by association between the U.S.S.R. behind Mossadegh, the major Western powers sympathetic to the Shah.

Before leaving Teheran I had had what I well realized could turn out to be my final meeting with the Boscoe brothers. We would, of course, be in constant communication, but to maintain absolute security we were planning to avoid any face-to-face meetings. If and when our agreed-upon mission, to help restore the Shah to his rightful power, should be completed, they planned to drop completely out of my life. Our people might stay in occasional touch with them, but that too would fade. Younger Boscoe, the newspaperman, either had never been in contact with, or was careful to stay away from, the foreign correspondents and the few members of the Iranian press whom I was likely to see. The older brother, as I have said, was a lawyer but solely with Iranian clients. The few Persian lawyers I knew, most of whom worked for their government, were involved with the American government and with various Western companies active in Iran which were of interest to me. (Today, if I were to meet one of the Boscoe brothers, I am sure I would not recognize whichever one of them it might be. Nor would their real names mean anything to me.)

In the summer of 1951 we had reviewed the situation, the needs for possible action and our chances of success. The conviction that Mossadegh would come to power, would be appointed P.M., had been proven true. As we had anticipated, the alliance between him and the Russian-dominated Tudeh was taking on a threatening shape. The mood of most of the mullahs was still definitely anti-Shah, but we could see the possibility—a hopeful one—that as Mossadegh and the Tudeh grew closer, the mullahs would turn away. Where could they turn except to the Shah? They could be neutral, could stay out of things, in effect say, "A curse on both your houses." This is what the Boscoes had foretold. I was less certain, thinking it possible that they would feel forced to choose and would, even though reluctantly, choose the Shah over Communism.

"You don't really understand the mullahs," the older brother had said, perhaps with good reason. "They see nothing incompatible between their religion and what they know of Communism. They judge it to be a political, not an ideological, force. If the Russians show their hand too much, that will certainly put them off. But even that wouldn't necessarily make them pro-Shah. My own guess is that they may end up unhappily neutral, regarding both sides of the struggle as equally bad, as equally opposed to what they believe in. If the Soviets are skillful, and conceal their involvement, I would guess they would stick with Mossadegh. The Russians would really have to expose themselves to scare them off him, and even then I doubt that they would be scared all the way to the other side."

Again, I expressed my doubts. And now when the crunch was coming, we could still not be sure which of us was right. They undoubtedly knew the mullahs far better than did I, but even they—modern activists that they were—had little firsthand contact with the old-school religious leaders. We both felt that the mullahs were losing their hold on the educated classes, but these were yet a small segment of Iran. However, we all clung to what was, after all, our central point. If forced to choose between Mossadegh and the Shah, the Tudeh and the Shah or even the mullahs and the Shah, the people could make but one choice.

Nonetheless, I had wanted reassurance. "Tell me what you *really* believe about the reaction of the people."

Again, it was the older Boscoe who replied. With total confidence he told me, "Have no doubt about the people. They may respect a Prime Minister, a leading mullah, an army chief of staff. But the Shahanshah is their lord on earth just as Allah is above the earth. If, as you Americans put it"—he now, after one short visit, felt himself an authority on Americans—"if it comes to a crunch, have no doubt about it. If the situation, the reality can be made clear, the people will rush to support the monarch. All that must be done is to show them that the Prime Minister is trying to usurp the Shah's prerogatives. That sounds too formal," he acknowledged. He drew on another bit of slang he had picked up somewhere. "If the Prime Minister is trying to do the Shah in the eye, the people will rise up and clobber him."

I complimented Boscoe Senior on the fluency of his speech. "You've picked up another language—added American to your English, German, French, Farsi and whatever else you speak. You're a terrific linguist." There was, however, another question. What about the Army?

Here the younger Boscoe was the spokesman. "There are undoubtedly a few officers at the very top who are pro-Mossadegh and would stick with him even against H.I.M. General Riahi is certainly one, and I'm not sure how many others there are. But not many. And of 'other ranks' I'm sure there are damn few. The Shah, not General Riahi, not Dr. holier-than-God weep-along Mossadegh, is their Commander in Chief. If they can be made to understand that they have to choose, that they *must* pick the Shah or whoever else, then I'm absolutely certain that they'll rise with the people in support of H.I.M."

I had reached the same conclusion but was very glad to hear younger Boscoe reaffirm it so very strongly now. I had one more question.

"How will His Imperial Majesty react to a challenge from his Prime Minister to the royal prerogatives?"

Again it was young Boscoe who replied. "Don't worry about H.I.M." I wasn't worrying, but I wanted to see if these important associates were. "When the time comes he will act. No doubt he is concerned over the apparent fact that he has no foreign support. Obviously the Russians, and all the other countries ruled by or allied with them, are his enemies. He knows they support Mossadegh. What about the West? As you know, as we know, they *are* with him. But how can he tell? Look at the terrific reception Mossadegh was given in Washington. How can the Shah be sure, after that, that the U.S. will give him their backing? And the British, who are—whatever they may think—just about to be thrown out of Iran, why should he believe that they will come to his assistance? We hope you can find some way of convincing him, preferably not just of U.S. support but of British as well. We don't know just how you are going to arrange all this, but we tell you: It must be done!"

That, to use a phrase that linguist Boscoe would have appreciated, put the ball squarely in my court. I had pointed out, though without much conviction, that our undertaking was not yet approved by the United States government. I said nothing about the British; my Iranian allies would have to give me more time and the situation too. Affairs would have to develop to the point where my government could not avoid taking action, which they could see to be necessary, in support of the Shah. After all, the Democrats who had welcomed Mossadegh so warmly were still in office. I was sure, as far as anyone could ever be sure, that the Republicans would win the coming election. But that did not mean I could be confident of what they— whoever "they" were to be—would do. Who could tell?

So far I had not mentioned the project to any of my local representatives. Reynolds was due to leave soon, so I saw no point in involving him. Finally I decided to talk on general terms with the senior man, George Cuvier. He was leery even of discussing the possibility—the next year I was to find him even more so—but I was able to get his reaction to some of the key people and elements involved. Of Mossadegh he was distrustful but, in a curious way, still hopeful. H.I.M. he regarded with respect but, again curiously, with a certain hesitation and doubt. His most interesting contribution was on the Qashqais. (I had forgotten to ask the Boscoe brothers about any of the tribes and thought for a moment of going back to them. But the tribes were remote from their urban, professional lives.)

George had no strong views on other tribes. The Bakhtiari, despite their connection by marriage to H.I.M. through Empress Soraya, were has-beens in his opinion. The Kurds were interesting people; he liked them but saw no political role for them—or threat from them. But the Qashqais, they were a different kettle of fish altogether. He sought for words to express his distrust, even fear, of them. Menacing, vengeful, treacherous, ruthless, all of those and more. But what impressed him most of all was the hatred, the blazing hatred, they felt for the royal crown and its present wearer, Mohammed Reza Pahlavi. His father, after all, had tried to cut them down, and only the Russian/British occupation, together with their skillful fooling of the Germans, had saved them.

"Mark my words, Kim, those four Qashqai brothers,

the ruling Khans, are true terrors. You met them some years ago. They're smooth. At that time, I guess, they were playing a waiting game and may have sweet-talked you a bit. But now they sense their day is coming and they can hardly contain themselves. Don't go anywhere near them if you become identified with the Shah. They'll tear you limb from limb!"

I did remember the Qashqais quite vividly, especially Khosro Khan, and could well believe what George was saying. I would watch my step. Meanwhile, I had inquired about Americans and other foreigners in the neighborhood of Teheran. Our embassy people, most of them, I already knew. Ambassador Henry Grady was about to be replaced by my old friend Loy Henderson, and another old friend, John Stutesman, was also due to leave. Of the British, soon to be evicted, I knew several—the Ambassador, his counselor and of course my friend Gordon Somerset. In the French, Italian and German embassies I had a few friends, most of whom had served in Washington. The foreign business community was small in those days. George, speaking French as fluently as he did English, which was exceptionally fluently, knew most of them (he was a most gregarious character, which was both an advantage and a danger in his line of work). I was acquainted with only a few businessmen, mostly Americans, and one Japanese whom I had sat next to on an airplane flying from Calcutta to Teheran. He was an attractive chap, and we had kept in touch.

Then there was the foreign press. To the best of my recollection there had been no American reporters stationed regularly in Iran. Most of them covered any major news stories from Beirut or even from Athens. But from March 1953 on, as the crisis was clearly building up, a number visited from time to time. Of those I remembered hearing the name of Kennett Love, the *New York Times* correspondent, whom I had known in Cairo. If AJAX succeeded, we could expect a flood of them. But now they were represented by "stringers," such as the young Iranian with whom Polly and I had traveled by car from Shiraz to Teheran in 1947, after our visit to the four Qashqai brothers. Then I was a writer myself and happy to associate with others of my craft. But since returning to government service I had, with a good deal of luck to help me, avoided them like the plague.

When I could think of nothing more to ask George Cuvier, I went back up the mountainside, where I gathered son Kermit and the Reynoldses, Senior and Junior. We had taken off for the isolation of the Caspian Sea, thence to Tabriz and over the border to Turkey. From Erzerum we went on to Trabzon and along that yet little-traveled Black Sea coast, where the road was so pitted and pocked that we did well to cover ten miles in an hour. It took us three full days to motor from Trabzon to Sinop, just about 250 miles. After that, with Ankara to the south of us, we cut down to join the main road to Istanbul. There we were back in civilization, in touch with the world. Happily no messages were waiting, from anywhere, for me. Kermit and I said farewell to the Reynoldses and flew off to join my brother Dirck in Madrid. Dirck, an efficiently harebrained young man, took us to the festival at Pamplona, where we ran in front of the bulls (in true Hemingway fashion) and watched, with less excitement, some rather poor bullfights. I found it all surprisingly relaxing.

"Nothing happens without a cause. Everything
has a cause and is necessary!"
Leucippus (c. 450 B.C.)

I was sufficiently
with this world—the world of July 1953—so that I did
board my plane at Rome. But basically, psychologically, I was still reliving the recent past; I was back in
Istanbul at the end of July 1951. And I was remembering what I had not learned then, that Harriman, on
leaving Teheran about two weeks after the Tudeh
stoning provoked by the Boscoe brothers, had flown to
London. Before going on to Washington he had persuaded the British Labour government to send a
delegation of very senior officials to Teheran. It was
led by Sir Richard Stokes, Lord Privy Seal and
Minister of Materials. The mission had two other

cabinet ministers as members. Dean Acheson reported that his friend the British Ambassador described
Stokes as a "'bluff, genial, and hearty man,' without
experience in dealing with the Near Eastern mentali-
ty. This," Acheson noted with his customary acerbity,
"proved to be sheer flattery."*

The negotiations begun by Stokes did limp on for
some time. The British had concluded that they must
accept the *principle* of nationalization, though its
application remained most difficult to agree upon.
The Shah himself felt that the essential differences
between the AIOC and the Iranian government were
resolvable, but Mossadegh would not listen. He was
convinced that if he refused any major adjustment in
terms, the British would have to give in.

This dangerous miscalculation was recognized by
the Shah.** "When our oil industry had been nationalized and Mossadegh had first come to power, the
British government and the Company had quickly seen
the writing on the wall. Completely reversing their
former policy, they formally accepted the principle of
nationalization. . . . Think of the economic miseries
and political perils that the people of my country
would have been spared if Mossadegh had been willing
to enter into rational negotiations."

Nonetheless, the news did give us some faint hope
that things might be worked out. I called upon the
Iranian Ambassador in Washington. He was an extremely astute gentleman by the name of Nasrollah
Entezam, completely loyal to the Shah. Mossadegh
had him replaced in 1952 by one of his own followers,
Allahyeh Saleh, who lasted just one year. Then Entezam returned. This occasion, in early September
1951, was our first meeting. Later ones, I must admit,

*Acheson, *op. cit.*, p. 509.
**Mission for My Country, p. 92.

were happier. Now we were both mystified and worried about what was happening in Teheran. We fenced politely, neither of us ready to admit our concern, but each of us gradually confessing to our unease. After a certain amount of "Mr. Ambassador, what do you think . . ." and "Mr. Roosevelt, what do *you* think . . ." we reached a degree of frankness.

"Honestly, sir," I admitted, "I simply cannot get any clear picture, either from friends in Iran or government colleagues here, of just what is happening. Can you tell me anything? Preferably," I added, "something encouraging."

He smiled but not very happily. "At best it is a very difficult situation. I will ask you to protect what I tell you, and I will speak quite openly. Premier Mossadegh is gaining strength and confidence. For the time being, everything goes his way. I do not trust his intentions toward the Shah, and I am quite certain that as soon as he thinks he can safely do it, he will replace me. Of course H.I.M. must appoint ambassadors, but at this point I don't think he will—or should—oppose the P.M.'s wishes.

"However," he went on with emphasis, looking at me gravely, "I do not, I *cannot*, believe that this will continue. Sooner or later Dr. M. will overreach himself, become too obviously an instrument being used by enemies of Iran. Surely I need not identify them to you. When that happens, the tide will turn—very suddenly." I had been glad to have my own belief reconfirmed by such an astute Iranian.

But events were not moving well in Teheran. The British Labour government's mission made no progress in their talks, which lasted from August 6 to 22. The British had begun by declaring their readiness to accept the principle of nationalization. But this was dependent on Iranian willingness to pay "adequate" compensation and to charter a British company to handle the technical aspects of production. The Iranians compromised by offering to hire British technicians individually rather than as part of an organized unit. That the U.K. delegation accepted on the condition that a British general manager be given a supervisory executive role. The Iranians rejected this, and the talks broke down. I remember going to see George McGhee at the State Department to compare notes. McGhee continued mildly optimistic and hopeful. The reasoning behind his optimism entirely escaped me, and I said so—I hope not too aggressively. He simply smiled and sent me on my way. I went again to the Iranian Embassy, but they were no better informed than I. Our own embassy in Teheran, and my senior representative Cuvier, were reporting copiously, but I did not find their reports enlightening. There was, as one of my colleagues put it most succinctly, a "mishmash" in Teheran.

After he had sent the British delegation packing, Mossadegh made a great many fiery orations. Sharp words, alternately threatening and cajoling, were exchanged with London, mostly through the U.S. Embassy in Teheran, which repeated them to our embassy in Britain and to Washington. In September 1951 the Iranian Prime Minister notified all British employees of AIOC that they were to be expelled from Iran. On September 27 of that year he instructed Iranian troops to occupy the Abadan refinery. At first the British seemed likely to reply by force. They had sent a cruiser, the *Mauritius*, to join other smaller vessels and to lie off the Iranian shore. It required U.S. pleas, plus Soviet threats, to dissuade the Labour government from having the *Mauritius* shell Abadan. This was certainly a Churchillian reaction, but Churchill was not himself to be in power for another month. By that time the feelings against such an action by England were well established and painfully convincing. The British staff of AIOC was evacuated, as Mossadegh had instructed, and the evacuation was a lugubrious ceremony.

As the official historian of AIOC, Henry Longhurst wrote:*

On the morning of October 4, 1951, the party assembled before the Gymkhana Club, the centre of so many of the lighter moments of their life in Persia, to embark for Basra in the British cruiser *Mauritius*. Some had their dogs, though most had had to be destroyed; others carried tennis rackets and golf clubs; the hospital nurses and the indomitable Mrs. Flavell who ran the guest house and three days previously had intimidated** a Persian tank commander with her parasol for driving over her lawn, were among the party, and the Rev. Tyrie had come sadly from locking up in the little church the records of those who had been born, baptised, or had died in Abadan. . . . The ship's band, "correct" to the end, struck up the Persian national anthem and the launches began their shuttle service . . . The cruiser *Mauritius* steamed slowly away up river with the band playing, the assembled company lining the rails and roaring in unison the less printable version of "Colonel Bogey." Next day Ross and Mason [the two senior officials] drove away. The greatest single overseas enterprise in British commerce had ground to a standstill.

Behind them they left what can simply be described as one *hell* of a mess. There were pipelines through which the pumping stations were no longer moving oil. The refineries were closed down. Crude oil, which no tankers were moving, flooded the tank farms. Seventy thousand Iranian employees, who had been paid about eight million dollars a month, were still theoretically

Adventure in Oil: The Story of British Petroleum. London: Sidgwick & Jackson, 1959, pp. 143–44.

**So Longhurst asserts.

on the payroll. But how was Mossadegh to pay them? The government didn't have the money, had in fact other obligations equally pressing which it had no possible hope of fulfilling. For the British the situation was almost as bad. The AIOC had been one of the United Kingdom's principal earners of foreign exchange and had supplied also the bulk of its domestic petroleum requirements. Now, at a time when their dollar reserves were already dangerously low, the U.K. would have to buy the oil it needed from other sources who would demand "hard" currency for payment. Needless to say, this awkward situation did nothing to help the Labour government in the elections which were soon to come.

In October 1951 Mossadegh went to New York to attend a United Nations Security Council meeting. The British had appealed the case to the International Court of Justice at the Hague,* which on July 5 had made a provisional ruling ordering maintenance of the *status quo* pending final settlement. Later the United Kingdom submitted a resolution to the Security Council which, if adopted, would have required Iran to conform to this provisional ruling. Mossadegh spoke out in his usual eloquent and often tearful fashion against the British effort and against the authority of the court to claim any jurisdiction. The UN Security Council declined to accept responsibility in the matter, which left the International Court without guidance and therefore without any course of action to pursue.

His mission accomplished, Prime Minister Mossadegh then went to Washington for a medical check-up and by no means incidentally for meetings with Presi-

---

*On May 26, 1951. See Donald N. Wilber, *Iran Past and Present*, Princeton, 1958 (a revised edition of the 1948 book), p. 114. Other histories of Iran during this period are, many of them, confused and confusing on the episode.

dent Truman and Secretary of State Acheson. From the first moment he saw the Premier, Acheson reports,* Mossadegh became for him the character Lob in James Barrie's play *Dear Brutus*. Lob is described by Barrie as "very small, and probably no one has ever looked so old except some newborn child. . . . He enters portentously, his hands behind his back, as if every bit of him, from his domed head to his little feet, was the physical expression of deep thoughts within him, then suddenly he whirls around to make his guests jump. This amuses him vastly, and he regains his gravity with difficulty." From his own words, it is easy to see why Acheson made the comparison. He depicts Mossadegh as "small and frail, with not a shred of hair on his billiard-ball head; a thin face protruding into a long beak of a nose flanked by two bright, shoe-button eyes. His whole manner and appearance was birdlike and he moved quickly and nervously as if he were hopping about on a perch. His pixie quality showed in instantaneous transformations."

When Dean met him at the Union Station in Washington, he watched a bent old man hobble down the platform, supporting himself on a stick and leaning on his son's arm. But spotting Acheson at the gate, he dropped the stick, broke away from his son and came skipping along ahead of his group to greet the greeters. He had, Dean discovered, "a delightfully childlike way of sitting in a chair with his legs tucked under him, making him more a Lob character than ever." Acheson recalls a meeting at the Presidential guest residence, Blair House, when Mossadegh purposefully dropped his mood of gay anticipation. Leaning toward Mr. Truman, looking suddenly old and pathetic, he said in trembling tones, "I am speaking for a very poor

*Acheson, *op. cit.*, pp. 503 *et seq.*

country—a country all desert—just sand, a few camels, a few sheep . . ." Acheson interrupted to observe that with all its sand *and* oil, Iran was rather like Texas. Mossadegh broke into a delighted laugh and the whole act had to be abandoned. His gambit had not worked, but no one was more amused than he. I cannot help feeling that if Dean had not pointed out the ridiculousness of the P.M.'s approach, President Truman would have taken it, as Mossadegh intended him to, quite seriously.

The Secretary of State's final comment is typically Achesonian. "In a service often trying I found compensation, indeed joy, in the qualities of friendly colleagues, of hostile combatants, and sometimes of neutral freebooters like Mossadegh.* Only bores were insufferable." But Mossadegh's self-defeating quality, Acheson recognized, was his inability to understand that the same passions he excited to support his position did in fact restrict his choice, leaving only extreme solutions possible. The United States (for which one can read Acheson himself) was slow to realize that Mossadegh was "essentially a rich, reactionary, feudal-minded Persian inspired by a fanatical hatred of the British and a desire to expel them and all their works from the country regardless of cost."** He was an actor and a great gambler. He would rant, weep real tears, fall fainting in the Majlis. Convinced that any damages the British oil company could prove in a court of law would be well exceeded by Iranian counterclaims, he told the Americans that nationalization could cost Iran nothing. Acheson concluded: "This unique character truly sowed the wind and reaped the whirlwind."

---

*It is interesting that Acheson should describe Mossadegh as a *neutral* freebooter.

**Acheson, *op. cit.*, p. 504.

From his high-level talks in Washington, Dr. Mossadegh returned home to a hero's welcome in Teheran on November 23.*

In the meantime, while Dr. Mossadegh was in the U.S., the Tories had won the election in Great Britain. Churchill was now Prime Minister, Anthony Eden his Foreign Secretary. Their inclination was, to put it mildly, not toward a temperate Iranian policy. If gunboat diplomacy had not already been tried, and thwarted, they would certainly have attempted it. As it was, I do not think they took very seriously the diplomatic efforts required of them for appearance's sake. They were already turning their thoughts to other methods of coping with the situation.

In January 1952 Prime Minister Mossadegh took a further step toward the breaking of all relations with the British. He ordered the British consulates in Iran to shut down. In mid-February Hossein Fatemi, then editor of the National Front paper *Bakhtar Emruz*, later Foreign Minister, was seriously wounded by a young member of the Fedayun-I-Islam. For more than half a year thereafter, U.S. efforts to keep the talks between Iran and the British going did achieve a bare minimum of success. Communications were exchanged between the two conflicting parties, mostly through Washington, but absolutely no progress was made. In September, Mossadegh had had enough of these efforts. He broke diplomatic relations with the United Kingdom and expelled all the remaining British from Iran. Just before that an American oilman— Mr. W. Alton Jones, president of Cities Service— appeared in Iran to negotiate a role for his company in

*One chronologically impossible if psychologically apt story has Dr. M. returning to Iran via Cairo, where he was given a "hero's welcome" by Gamal Abdel Nasser. This is from George Lenczowski's *The Middle East in World Affairs*, Cornell University Press, Ithaca, New York, 1952, p. 188. Actually Naguib and Nasser did not take power until July 1952, and Farouk, no friend to Mossadegh, was still King.

foreign distribution and sales of the nationalized Iranian oil. His known friendship with President Eisenhower alarmed the British and briefly encouraged Mossadegh. But the latter became ever more stubborn. Jones got nowhere and withdrew just before the total rupture of Iranian–British relations.

In concluding his remarks on Iran, Acheson, I recalled, jumps ahead to the summer of 1953 and has only this to comment: "The alternative to Mossadegh for which the British had been looking had been found.* But, as the Iron Duke had said of Waterloo, it was a 'damned near thing.'" Dean concludes, "Once again one reflects on Oxenstiern's question: 'Dost thou not know, my son, with how little wisdom the world is governed?'"**

In the fall of 1952, immediately after the British expulsion from Iran, Churchill and Eden turned to what they had probably had in mind from shortly after their coming into office. When I was on my way home from Teheran in November 1952, British Intelligence approached me as I stopped in London. For the first time I met Mr. (later Sir John) Cochran, who served as spokesman for the group. What they had in mind was nothing less than the overthrow of Mossadegh. Furthermore, they saw no point in wasting time by delay. They wanted to start immediately. I had to explain that the project would require considerable clearance from my government and that I was not entirely sure what the results would be. As I told my British colleagues, we had, I felt sure, no chance to win approval from the outgoing administration of Truman and Acheson. The new Republicans, however, might be quite different. They brushed aside my reservations and proposed that we have at least a thorough prelimi-

*He refers to General Zahedi.
**Acheson, *op. cit.*, p. 685.

nary talk right then and there. I was dealing at this time only with Cochran, his principal lieutenant Henry Montague and with his recently returned head of the Iranian office, Gordon Somerset. They had already sketched out a plan of battle and, while they recognized that we might have political problems, they could see no other reason for delay. We did take the time to go into their battle plan in some detail. In later talks, the number of participants on both sides would be substantially increased. But at the beginning it was just the four of us. To my considerable surprise, Cochran himself participated vigorously in each discussion.

What the British had, in effect, was a detailed plan. Personally I did not see how that kind of plan could bear much relation to what might develop in the actual course of an operation. However, there was no point in arguing it, and I listened to their outlined project with considerable interest. Until the U.S. had committed itself with them to the undertaking, they understandably had no intention of disclosing the identity of their allies. But it appeared from the outline that they considered they had some highly competent, well-connected "friends" to contribute. They made it plain at the beginning that they expected to be working with H.I.M., not against him. Their principal agents were described as having very close relations with the palace. This was an obvious advantage and one from which we could well benefit, if we were to undertake the overthrow of Mossadegh. Later, as they elaborated on the contacts and competence of these agents, I began to worry that they might be referring to the Boscoe brothers. It was not till they reached the point of disclosure that I could be confident that they were not.

On the Army, their estimate was essentially the same as that of the Boscoes and myself. This was fine—unless our estimates came from the same source. Riahi, the commander-in-chief, was pro-Mossadegh, and an indeterminate number of senior officers might be expected to support him. But the junior officers, the noncoms and the enlisted men as a whole, were judged to be pro-Shah—by them as well as by us. I broke down their estimates into the same categories that we had earlier discussed in Teheran. They were rather more optimistic about the mullahs than our brothers, or even I, had been. On the college faculties and students they were as pessimistic as we. And on the people at large we were also in substantial agreement. All in all, so long as we were not going to the same well-head to quench our thirst for knowledge, this was very reassuring.

It was also most fortunate that both the British and ourselves operated on a strict "need to know" basis. Kim Philby, son of the St. John ("Sinjun") Philby of Arabian fame and now a refugee in Moscow, had, thank goodness, no such need. When in 1949 he had come to Washington as the British liaison officer with CIA I soon became suspicious of him because of his intimacy with Guy Burgess, who lived in his house. Guy was close to being an alcoholic if he was not actually one. He *was* working for the Soviets, and drink made him indiscreet enough to betray it. He and Donald Maclean, who had also been recruited by the Russians, were both warned of their danger in the nick of time. Philby got word to them and enabled them to flee to the safe haven of Moscow. A CIA colleague of mine, the unidentified "hero" of a novel by Aaron Latham called *Orchids for Mother*, and I were the first to become suspicious of Philby himself. Later these suspicions spread. Philby was "retired" by his service. He went to live in Beirut, but as the evidence against him mounted, he too sought sanctuary in the U.S.S.R.

There he apparently does odd jobs for the KGB. He has also corresponded with the author of a recent book on John Foster, Allen and Eleanor Dulles.* He is surprisingly kind in his comments on me, claiming to have dubbed me "the quiet American" five years before Graham Greene wrote a novel of the same name. I am "a courteous, soft-spoken Easterner with impeccable social connections, well-educated rather than intellectual, pleasant and unassuming as host and guest. An equally nice wife. In fact, the last person you would expect to be up to the neck in dirty tricks." Thank *you,* Mr. Philby!

He goes on to say that he was in London during the Iranian crisis and had no contact with me at that time. To this, my reply is more properly, Thank God—and my naturally suspicious mind.

To return to London in November 1952, Mr. Cochran and his associates assured me that Foreign Minister Eden** and—with special vehemence—Prime Minister Churchill were fully behind their plan. I remembered then my own first meeting with Churchill. This had been at the end of 1941, less than three weeks after Pearl Harbor. He had flown the Atlantic to meet with FDR soon after the Japanese attack. My wife and I were invited to Christmas lunch at the White House, where FDR, cigarette holder as usual jutting from his mouth, and Churchill, wreathed in smiles, toasted the table guests, the world and each other in champagne—and equally bubbly optimism. This was a full year before their meeting with Stalin in Teheran and a bit over a year before my first visit to Iran.

Some months earlier I had met a European diplomat

---

*Leonard Mosley, *Dulles: A Biography of Eleanor, Allen and John Foster Dulles and Their Family Network*, New York: Dial Press, 1978.

**See Eden, *op. cit.,* p. 67.

who had served as number two in his country's Teheran embassy from early 1947 until late 1952 and who I still cannot name. With surprising frankness he told me how badly he, and many others of his diplomatic colleagues, had misjudged the Shah, Qavam and, in due course, Dr. Mohammed Mossadegh as well.

When he arrived in Iran he was advised by his own Ambassador that until September 1946—to quote him exactly—"Qavam could have kicked the Shah off the throne at any time he wanted to. My boss had been much concerned about Qavam's personal ambitions, and the danger that he might seek Tudeh and Soviet help to do the job."

He repeated a description his Ambassador had given him of meeting, often most informally, with the Shah. "H.I.M., he thought, used him as a rhetorical sounding board. Once, with an ironical smile, the ruler remarked that a member of his family, probably Princess Ashraf, had asked sharply whether he were man or mouse. Did the Ambassador think, as the Shah suspected, that he should simply stay in his palace at Saadabad, enjoying his pleasant gardens, his dogs and horses, his tennis—and do *nothing* about the tragic situation of his country? This when Pishevari, the Azerbaijani Communist leader, was about to steal the most important province of Iran!"

The Ambassador missed what I now recognize to be the irony of the question. But he did notice the astonishment with which his reply was received. What he said was: Yes. Qavam had assumed responsibility for the negotiations with Pishevari. The Shah would only get himself mixed up in a partisan quarrel if he tried to intervene. It was not a "king's business" to meddle in politics.

As the Ambassador reported the incident to my friend, the Shah was not—in his opinion—strong enough to succeed. "And if by some miracle he did, where would he ever stop? My boss was obviously looking at Iran as if it were our own country, which had been a constitutional monarchy for centuries before we finally got rid of our king. I see now, though I didn't see it then, that H.I.M. was already outgrowing respect for the 'lessons' which Western ambassadors—mine, yours and others—were preaching to him. Iran was *not* a Western republic; he must see it as it was, live with it as it was.

"But my ambassador did note that, 'oddly enough,' as he put it, the Qashqai uprising in September 1946* did swing the tide in the Shah's favor. It did not look favorable in any way. The revolt was settled by agreement between the Qashqai khans and Qavam that they could keep their arms in return for supporting him in the upcoming election. What it did additionally, however, was to halt the Tudeh advance into south Persia. And it was soon after that that Pishevari and the Russians badly overestimated their strength.** They made demands, 95 percent of which Qavam might have persuaded the Shah to accept. But Pishevari insisted that Azerbaijani officers who had deserted the army during the November 1945 revolt be readmitted with substantial promotions. This the Shah absolutely refused. Pishevari returned to Tabriz in a huff, one of several incredible blunders which can be explained only by Soviet overconfidence. The Shah's steady rise in popularity began from that moment."

The conversation then moved forward to the case of Dr. Mossadegh. At the end of 1951, almost a year before my friend was to be replaced, his Ambassador was reassigned. As his departure time grew near, he

*Described on p. 78.
**Already mentioned on pp. 61–67.

reviewed the field of battle with his number two, about to become *chargé d'affaires*. "He admitted without reservation that by then it was clear that the Shah did not like Mossadegh's National Front. Nor did he believe that nationalizing the oil would mean progress for his country. But he had not, up to that time, made his opposition to Mossadegh plain, even to those elements in the Majlis on whose support he could count. My ambassador observed cautiously that he doubted whether Mossadegh was truly grateful for the Shah's attitude! Obviously H.I.M. distrusted the venality of Mullah Kashani, the opportunism of Makki, and the radicalism of Baghai.* Most important, he was certain of the hostility of Russia and quite uncertain of what support he could hope for from the West. How, at that moment, could he commit himself to unequivocal opposition to the Mossadegh government?"

After his chief had left, my friend commented, he himself was told of one other interesting sign of the Shah's strength. "Some embassy, I'm not sure which, organized a small, informal poll among laborers in south Teheran. It was not big enough to prove much, resting on brief interviews with only fifty local workers. But of these, nine-tenths affirmed themselves to be royalists, the remaining four or five convinced Communists. Even then, I could hardly fail to recognize its meaning. To remove the Shah, as Mossadegh was already threatening to do, would create confusion. As far as the urban and peasant masses are concerned, the symbol of the monarch is the heart of central government. Remove it, and what have you left?" I could see the question, I could even see what the answer had to be, but I could not see *how* it could be. I was about to show him how.

*Abol Qasem Kashani led the opposition among the mullahs; Hussein Makki was the man who turned the valve to start the flow of oil at Abadan; and Mozaffar Baghai created the Toilers' Party to attract workers to the National Front.

CHAPTER
7

"He who has a choice has trouble."
Dutch proverb

"Convictions are more dangerous to truth than lies."
Friedrich Nietzsche (1878)

"If you can't make a man think as you do,
make him do as you think."
Author unknown

Some months earlier—in November 1952, to be precise—I stopped off in London on my way home from Teheran. The British had been thrown out of Iran, in bits and pieces, during the year, and they had finally severed diplomatic relations. From the British point of view, my arrival in London was perfectly timed. The Foreign Office got hold of me immediately, introduced me to Mr. Cochran and his associates, and they "popped the question."

It was a bit early for us to take their suggestion seriously. Truman and Acheson had, as we have seen, been rather charmed by Mossadegh on his visit to the U.S. in October 1951. Allen Dulles and I might well be in sympathy with our cousins, as indeed we were. However, we had to wait for the U.S. elections—which had just taken place—to produce the actual changes in office before we could move.

But early in 1953, before the Republican inauguration and before "Beedle" Smith had been moved over to the State Department—Dulles' enemies said it was to make room for Allen as Director of the CIA—I had taken the shuttle bus up to his office to have a chat with the general. Actually, "chat" is a deceptively relaxed word; "confrontation" would be more appropriate.

"When are those blanking British coming to talk to us? And when is our goddam operation going to get underway?" he had asked in his usual aggressive fashion.

"As soon after Inauguration Day as you and JFD can see them," I answered. "They're every bit as eager to get going as you are. But we still have considerable studying to do before we'll be sure, reasonably sure, that we can pull it off."

Beedle grunted. "Of course we can," he said irritably. "Pull up your socks and get going, young man."

"There's still a long way to go," I commented mildly—or, you could say, diffidently. "We've got to be sure that Mossadegh is as vulnerable as we think he is, that he is associated in the eyes of army and people with the Tudeh–Russian team and that the Shah does in fact have the backing countrywide that we believe he does."

Beedle grunted again. "You'd better drag your tail over there and make sure, damn soon, damn sure!"

"As soon as the meeting's over, I'll do another survey. We'll have to put together an operational plan that the top people here and in London can approve."

"You won't have any trouble in London." Beedle practically never laughed, but he gave me a thin grin to indicate amusement. "They'll jump at anything we propose. And I'm sure you can come up with something sensible enough for Foster to O.K. Ike will agree." I felt that he was about to say, "with whatever we tell him," but he bit that back. Instead, he finished, "I'm sure you'll come up with something reasonable and he'll agree." He grinned again, sourly. And that was that.

To review briefly the major developments related to our undertaking: After the assassination of Prime Minister Razmarah by the "Crusaders of Islam" in March 1951, Hussein Ala had succeeded him. In May, Mossadegh took his place and made the visit I have described to the U.S. in October of that year. On July 13, 1952, he had his first major clash with the Shah. His demand for extraordinary powers was refused, but the naming of his successor, that old relic of past days, Ahmed Qavam, met with violent rioting. On July 22, H.I.M. felt compelled to reappoint Mossadegh and comply with his demand.

In September 1952 Truman and Churchill sent their last joint note to Mossadegh proposing a formula for an oil settlement. Mossadegh rejected this, and on October 22 he broke off relations with Great Britain. I was in Teheran just a week later and stopped in London on my way home for what turned out to be the first discussion of an anti-Mossadegh operation with the British. In January 1953 the Majlis granted Mossadegh an extension of his emergency powers. The Shah approved this. "I wanted," H.I.M. has written, "to give him every opportunity to develop a constructive oil policy."* Now Eisenhower took President Truman's place in sending joint notes with Churchill. Churchill was certainly going through the routine for appearance's sake, and I doubt very much whether President Eisenhower—or more certainly Secretary of State Dulles—was really hopeful of any prospect of success. In fact, Mossadegh rejected their proposals as he had all previous offers.

In February the Prime Minister, increasingly closely allied with the Tudeh and, at one remove through them, with the Soviets, made his first effort to get the Shah to leave Iran. Mass demonstrations of loyalty to the monarchy, however, encouraged H.I.M. to stay. "By mid-1953 there was a definite change in the temper of the nation. Many of Mossadegh's followers had deserted him."** June saw a further development. President Eisenhower warned the Prime Minister that unless the oil controversy was settled, the United States could not increase its aid to Iran as Mossadegh was insisting be done. (Mossadegh's obvious objective was to substitute increased U.S. aid for the elimination of his oil income.) The Prime Minister replied that the U.S. *must* provide additional aid to prevent Iran from falling to the Communists. Yet at the same time he was daily letting the Communists grow stronger. "I think," the Shah observed later, "the American authorities were fully aware of these inconsistencies but naturally felt it was up to us Persians to solve our political problems. That is exactly what we proceeded to do."*** H.I.M. of course at that time had no idea of the American decision to support him.

As recounted earlier, the British stopped me on my way home and proposed the operation against Mossa-

*Mission for My Country, p. 95.
**Ibid., p. 97.
***Ibid., pp. 98–99.

degh. After the new Administration had come into office, British Intelligence paid us a visit in Washington that I will describe in some detail later. Thereafter my visits to Iran were made with more confidence and more sense of purpose—an understanding that in all likelihood we would proceed with the operation.

Between the election and Eisenhower's inauguration, Ambassador Henderson had returned to Teheran. He resumed his conversations with Mossadegh and continued to negotiate until February 1953. Once, he tells me, our Ambassador had asked Mossadegh to confirm his (Loy's) memory of a conversation in the preceding year from his "black book." This was a notebook in which he kept records of most of the conversations he had—certainly all of those with Henderson. Loy reports, with some amusement at Mossadegh's obvious guile, that the old man did produce a black book. But Loy, who was a very sharp observer, saw that it was a different black book from the one in which the P.M. had earlier been taking notes. He searched through it with all show of diligence, then reported to Loy that he had nothing that would confirm Loy's memory of the previous discussion. On this occasion, after Loy had left Mossadegh's bedroom, he saw a cane dangling from the banister as he started to go downstairs. He turned and looked to find a room next to the Prime Minister's with the door ajar. The cane was clearly that of the lame Foreign Minister Fatemi; despite Acheson's comments about Mossadegh's unwillingness to have anyone participate in his important conversations with foreigners, it was evident to Loy that Fatemi had been listening to their talk secretly in the adjoining room.

At this time, during late 1952 and early 1953, we assumed that Soviet embassies in Washington, London and Teheran were watching with interest what we, our British and our Iranian friends were up to. We could only hope that they had to watch from afar. Certainly they were ever more active in Iran. Their control over Tudeh leadership was growing stronger all the time. It was exercised often and, to our eyes, with deliberate ostentation. Rightly or wrongly, we felt the Soviets were flaunting their power, not so much to challenge as to intimidate us. Perhaps they thought we could be scared out of any attempt to put up a fight, to resist "manifest destiny," in Iran. We also found their manipulation of the good Dr. Mossadegh becoming ever more blatant. Clearly, they did not believe that we could respond effectively; in their estimation they had already won the day.

Perhaps, on the other hand, they were bluffing. In any case, if that really was their estimation we did not share it. The British, admittedly, struck us as dangerously overconfident. But those of our Iranian allies with whom we were already in contact, and we ourselves, looked to a favorable outcome when, at a time of our choosing, battle should be joined.

Twice, as I have already noted, in late 1952 and again in early 1953, British Intelligence journeyed to Washington to discuss the project. The first trip was purely for operational discussions—the CIA and our British friends. On our side Allen Dulles participated only briefly, Beedle Smith not at all. This was essentially because "Ike," who had chosen John Foster Dulles as Secretary of State almost immediately after the election, was making a secret trip to Korea at the end of November. Although JFD did not go, it was considered wise to keep him out of sight and this first Washington conference as strictly a working one. Therefore we did little more than review, in what seemed to me excessive detail, what Mr. Cochran, his colleagues and I had already discussed in London. The issue that divided us, the fact that British concern was basically about oil, the nationalization of AIOC, and their determination to regain ownership of the Iranian Oil Company, was still of great theoretical—one could almost say theological—importance. But as a practical matter it was becoming more and more irrelevant. If we both agreed, for whatever reason, that the circumstances required replacement of Prime Minister Mossadegh, the whys became academic. We made it clear that if we undertook the operation, and if it were successful, the Shah would be under *no* obligation. Not on petroleum, nor on anything else. The British had to agree; they really had no other choice.

So they returned to London to work further at their operational plan in spite of my mild comments on its probable lack of application. Objectives must be clearly understood by all parties. On the whys, we must agree. But as to the hows, I felt that no matter what interesting discussion of the subject we might have, a "flexible mind" was the real essential.

Early in February 1953 the British showed up in Washington again. We had our first get-together, with Allen participating, on Monday, February 3. This was just the operating elements; Sir Patrick Dean of the Foreign Office had come with the British mission but did not attend, nor did anyone from the State Department. We spent considerable hours in well-intended but, to my mind, rather aimless review. There was one new point, however. For the first time the British formally announced their intention to propose me as the "field commander" for the operation. To me, naturally, it seemed a very sensible proposal. Allen was, in his usual fashion, gruffly noncommittal. We agreed that the matter was one for discussion with Pat Dean, Beedle and Foster Dulles.

And of course when we did get together with them

we covered the old ground all over again. The British described the high capability of their principal agents, repeated their assessment of the Army—the top few leaders probably pro-Mossadegh but the bulk of the officers and essentially all noncoms and enlisted personnel loyal to H.I.M.—and of the loyalty of the people at large. They were still more hopeful on the mullahs than the Boscoe brothers had been, though personally I was inclined to share the British estimate. On the academic world we all continued to be pessimistic.

Cochran then gave a detailed outline of their operational plan, which, long as it seemed to me, I was sure I knew word for word by heart. Allen had already heard my views on this proposal and, bless him, repeated them, in his own words but without any meaningful change. Pat Dean listened gravely and said nothing. Beedle and JFD both grunted, which we all took to mean that they were in general agreement with what Allen had said. With them, the "flexible mind" won the day. Mr. C protested again that we *must* have precise guidelines to follow. But his remarks were received in more or less polite silence. Eventually he gave up.

Finally, the subject of the "field commander" was raised. This time Allen added cautious support to my nomination by the British. Beedle looked, in his sour way, gratified. Foster puffed on his cigarette rather as if it were a cigar and appeared to give the matter careful consideration. When he did speak it was to express some reservations. "We must remember that Kim is personally known to H.I.M. And he has a very prominent family name. If he could keep out of sight and not have to meet anyone who already knows him, I should think it would probably be all right."

He paused again. Allen's pipe and JFD's cigarette contributed jointly to the cloud of smoke. "Yes,"

Foster said finally and most judiciously, "I guess it would be O.K. But he will have to keep away from anyone who might know him. Especially the Shah."

Everyone agreed to his provisos, though I don't know how seriously the British took them. I certainly was not about to argue then, but I could see a possibility that the situation would change. We did know that H.I.M. was understandably uncertain of where the U.S. and the U.K. really stood. If he really needed convincing, it seemed to me that I had exactly the right credentials.

There was one final item for discussion at this high level and another that I intended to take up with the British visitors as soon as the present meeting was concluded.

"Gentlemen," I began most formally, "I would like to report to the State Department, the Foreign Office and our colleagues from Great Britain an important recent development. Lacking final approval for AJAX as yet, we have not been in direct contact with the Shah. But we have been talking to people close to him. Obviously we must settle upon whom it is we are supporting to replace Dr. Mossadegh, and obviously that is a decision to be made by H.I.M. Our Iranian colleagues advise us that his choice will, almost certainly, be General Fazlollah Zahedi."

There was a moment's silence. Foster and Beedle had no idea whom I was talking about. The British knew only too well.

"During World War Two, rightly or wrongly, the general was suspected by our allies of being pro-Nazi. He was arrested in Isfahan during the fall of 1941 by Colonel Fitzroy Maclean, author of a most imaginative book, *The Eastern Approaches*, about his travels in the Soviet Union just before the war, which describes the arrest. Zahedi was shipped off to Palestine, where he was interned. I do not know the general personally, but my Persian friends assure me that he does not retain any anti-British sentiments. He is, on the other hand, much opposed to the Soviet Union and alarmed by the Russian attempt to win control of his country."

Foster looked at me and then at our British visitors. In his deliberate drawl he asked, "Well, what do you think of that?" The British hesitated, but clearly it was up to the Foreign Office, represented by Pat Dean, to reply.

Pat cleared his throat. "This does come as a bit of a shocker," he said mildly. "I'm sure we shall have to refer it to London for comment." After a brief pause he added: "If this is what you and the Iranians feel is necessary, I don't see that we have much choice." He gave me a questioning look.

"I'm afraid that's right, Pat. Zahedi is not our selection, I promise you that. But we do think that the Shah must choose his own Prime Minister. And Fazlollah Zahedi appears to be his choice." I added once again that our Iranian contacts assured us, for what that was worth, that the general was not anti-British.

Foster Dulles pushed back his chair and lumbered to his feet. "I guess that's about all we can do now," he said gruffly. "Meeting adjourned!"

Some of us did not adjourn for long. I took our British friends directly back to Allen's office at 2430 E Street. There, in an effort to put them at ease, tea was served. (Probably the British would call it tea only out of politeness; it came in small tea bags and was not the best I've ever had.) Once they had got it down, I raised the question that had been plaguing me. Who *were* their principal representatives of whom they were so proud?

By this time our friends were satisfied that the

United States government was solidly in their camp, so after a brief private conference—I believe that Montague and Somerset wanted to make sure that Cochran knew who he was supposed to talk about—we had the long-awaited disclosure.

Mr. Cochran spoke most formally, as I had just done in Foster's office. "Our especial allies are a couple of top-flight fellows," he began.

I could not restrain myself. "They are not brothers, are they?" I asked eagerly.

He did not appreciate the interruption and looked at me with some severity. "Not at all." He gave their real names, which I will not repeat here. "We refer to them as Nossey and Cafron," he said stiffly. "They are, as I believe I have told you several times, quite exceptionally talented. Alert, attractive, full of life—lots of 'get up and go,' as you Americans say."

I hadn't said that for years, but I was in no mood to object. And here I must confess that I allowed professional scruples to overcome what moral scruples I might have felt. Now that I was sure that the Boscoes were truly ours and ours alone, I was not about to disclose them to the British. So I thanked Cochran warmly for his information, for which I was indeed thankful. "Of course we are not yet precisely sure which of our agents will be used in this undertaking. As soon as we do know, I shall advise you. It may well not be until I have arrived in Iran myself. We won't want, either of us, to place any unnecessary burden on limited communications facilities. So it's entirely possible that you will not get the information until after the affair is concluded."

Cochran and his lieutenants were, I believe, so anxious to "get the affair concluded" that they contentedly accepted my proposal.

Left: Lieutenant General Walter Bedell Smith

Below left: Secretary of State John Foster Dulles *(courtesy of Eleanor Dulles)*

Below right: Allen Welsh Dulles *(courtesy of Eleanor Dulles)*

Above left: Secretary of
State Dean Acheson
*(courtesy of David
Acheson)*

Above right: The author,
on the right, with
unidentified spy

Right: Translation of the
firman that orders
Fazlollah Zahedi to
form a new government

(The Royal Coat of Arms)

His Excellency Fazlollah Zahedi,

The situation of the country demands that We
appoint an experienced and well informed person to
take over the reins of the State. Being aware of
your merits and capabilities, We appoint you Prime
Minister, by this Firman, and ordain that you exert
adequate efforts to remove the present crisis and
raise the standard of living of the people.

Mohammad Reza Pahlavi

13 August, 1953

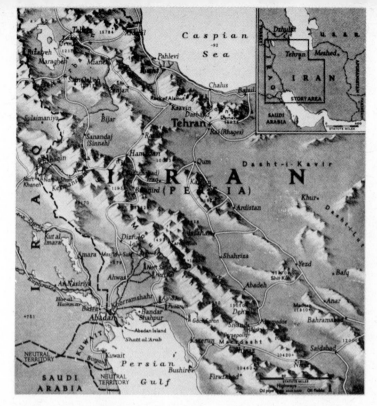

Above: Iran in 1953 *(drawn by Herbert E. Eastwood and Victor J. Kelly)*

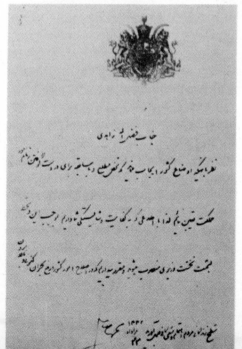

Left: A copy of the original document bearing the royal seal

Above: Demonstrators gather after the death of Joseph Stalin
(This and other pictures of events were given the author by a
friend who prefers to remain anonymous)

Left: An elderly woman cheers the Shah

Above left: Crowd storms the palace gates

Right: Demonstrators carried photographs of the Shah

Below: The Shah in prayer after his return to Teheran

Left: General Nassiry carried the Shah's order dismissing Mossadegh as Prime Minister and later arrested Mossadegh

Below: Former Prime Minister Mossadegh at his trial

Above: Mohamad Afshartus, chief of police under Mossadegh, assassinated in 1953

Below: Ebrahim Hakimi, three times Prime Minister

Above: Fazlollah Zahedi, who formed a new government as instructed by the Shah to replace Mossadegh

Below: Ali Amini, former Prime Minister

CHAPTER
8

"They say but little those
Who on the shore repose
Know of the woe that we
Bear on the stormy sea."
Saadi (d. 1291)

I made a number of visits to Iran, Beirut and London in the following months. Developments in Iran did continue to strengthen our belief that, despite surface appearances, the trend was really turning against Mossadegh. Our campaign against him was very low-key. Had we sought to have the newspapers, individuals or organizations commit themselves openly against their Prime Minister, and had they been foolish enough to do so, they would have been out of business immediately. However, if we were not too blatant about it, we and our Persian associates could underline Mossa-degh's alienation from the West, his increasing dependence on the Soviet Union and the obvious fact that if he continued to develop his personal regime as he was presently doing, there could be no continuing meaningful role for a monarch in Iran.

Meanwhile, in Washington, the Republicans were settling in—although the expression is altogether too mild to describe the way in which John Foster Dulles occupied the State Department. As in any new Administration, the top officials were anxious to improve upon the record of their predecessors and to show that their fresh outlook could significantly advance national interests. AJAX was sufficiently young and undeveloped so that Foster Dulles could quite properly claim it as his own.

One of the men most deeply involved in the early planning was George Cuvier, scheduled to be replaced in Iran in July 1953, just as our operation would be getting under way. I had earlier recalled my discussion with him following my last meeting with the Boscoe brothers. George was born in France, bilingual in French and English, and had picked up many French attributes. He was a person of great charm and cultivated wit. He had been with the counterespionage section of OSS during World War II and was an old hand on the intelligence side. What we called the political action side, however, was not his "dish of tea," as he was quite frank to admit. He took much interest in, and made great contributions to, the planning of the operation. However, he made it plain that he was glad that he would be out of the country before the action began. "Kim," he would say, "I am a very nervous man," and he would shrug his shoulders with typical Gallic expressiveness.

A couple of our planning sessions were held in

Beirut. The *maître d'* at the grill of the St. George Hotel turned out to be an old friend of Cuvier's from past days in Nice. So between long planning sessions in smoke-filled hotel rooms, with the radio going full blast as a security measure, we ate very well indeed.

I was well aware that George was a gourmet. I vividly remember him expounding on the finer points of cooking a fried egg. Someone asked him how you managed to get the yolk exactly in the middle of the white. George delicately extended his forefinger toward the center of his plate and smiled, including us in the secret with triumphant complicity and making delicate prodding gestures with the finger.

To return to the planning cycle: One of the features that made it not only bearable but actually enjoyable was the caliber of the individuals involved. I have already mentioned Roger Black, my bushy-haired professor friend, the intense-eyed "fanatic" with a high-pitched voice who had been quite innocently responsible for the enrollment of the Boscoe brothers. The professor had no further connection with the operation himself, and, after it was over, I think he must have suspected that the men he had referred on to us had played key roles in it. A sense of guilt, if no more than dubious guilt, would explain his passionate support of the National Front Movement in Iran even after it had long since ceased to exist. His resolute refusal to see any good in the post-1953 government, in the reforms introduced after Mossadegh's replacement, surprised his colleagues. They could not know, as some of us outside the academic world did, that he might feel a personal responsibility for the defeat of his revolutionary friends. In later years, until his death in 1967, I saw him from time to time. His eyes still gleamed fiercely; his articles in academic journals suggested no diminution of his support for "the cause."

Another Persian expert—an exceptionally thin man with a razor-sharp mind and less guilt-ridden than our other professorial friend—participated in a key role during preparation of much of the plan. He enjoyed it thoroughly and in return gave much enjoyment to his co-workers. Soon after I had first met him, he unnecessarily informed me that he had a "lithp." He was not, in appearance, anyone's idea of a secret operator, being very tall and *very* shy, with a diffident air and a modest, almost self-deprecating grin. His sense of humor was deceptively casual, and even after one knew him well, it was difficult to be sure whether he was serious or teasing in his proposals.

George Cuvier and I had a series of meetings with this consultant in Beirut. It was after one of these that I had dinner with some good friends, Farid and Yolande Nashashibi at their "castle" above the Beirut airport before returning to London. Farid, then Director of the Lebanese Sûreté, was well aware that something was up. He knew that whatever it was involved the British as well as the Americans, certainly in Iran and possibly in Egypt as well. While Yolande was being her usual charming self, he used all his professional technique to extract whatever secrets I might be harboring.

"Will you be going to Teheran soon?" he inquired guilelessly. "How long would you expect to be there? And who do you see there now?" When I gave him inconsequential replies, he asked about "my friend Mr. Nasser." As he plied me with questions I became increasingly concerned about the late hour. I was supposed to catch the Pan Am flight for London. Farid assured me that the plane would take off late and, anyway, that he would have me at the airport in plenty of time. I grew more and more suspicious and uneasy, finally insisting that I absolutely *must* go. Then Farid himself drove me to the airport.

I felt that our arrival was observed with unusual interest, even with relief. I was whisked out to the plane, skipping all the usual formalities, no check-out, no weighing of baggage, no inspection. The stewardesses were formidably cool, the pilots definitely hostile. It was not until after we were airborne that I discovered that Farid had been exercising his authority as Chief of Security to hold the plane for me. The Pan Am staff, quite naturally, had concluded that I was somehow to blame.

In late February 1953 I returned to spend a few more days in Beirut before taking the overland desert route on the Nairn bus to Baghdad. There I met Francis Granger, of our Iraqi station, with whom I drove on to Teheran. This was one of a series of interesting drives between Baghdad and Teheran in the years from 1947 through the mid-Fifties. Francis and I were caught in a snowstorm between Khanequin and Hamadan. We finally had to leave the main road to seek refuge in a small village, the only place we could find in all that desolate region which showed some sign of life.

There was indeed life, of a rather surprising sort. It was a Thursday evening, which is the equivalent of Christian Saturday night in Moslem countries, and we broke into the weekly village bridge game. The participants insisted on our joining it, perhaps because if we were to sleep it would have to be in the same room where the game was. Anyhow, wrapped in blankets and seated around tables with stoves underneath them to keep our nether quarters warm, we played till dawn. We went on to Teheran the next morning intellectually stimulated but physically worn.

I was in the Middle East at the time of Stalin's death, in March 1953. By this time our hopes for a favorable climate had grown even stronger; our plans were becoming more detailed and precise. On the same day that the Soviet Premier died, George Cuvier received a telephone call at his home. (As I have said, his "cover" was not the sturdiest I've known.) The caller did not identify himself but obviously knew not only Cuvier's name but that he was the intelligence representative for the area.

"Would you be able to meet me on the northwest corner of Kharia [avenue] Naderi and Kharia Razi in exactly one hour and fifteen minutes? You do not know me but I can recognize you. I shall pick you up in a dark-green Mercedes."

George, always curious and ready for adventure, agreed. At the appointed place and time, the Mercedes pulled up beside him, the driver reached across the front seat to open the door, and George climbed in next to him. The conversation began directly, with none of the usual politenesses and circumlocutions so much a part of Persian life at the time.

"Mr. Cuvier, General—" he named the commander of ground forces—"wishes to offer you his participation in a plan to replace Dr. Mossadegh." It was quite an offer. As George explained it to me later, it was clear that he had called on all his Gallic persuasiveness to explain that, sympathetic to the general's intention as he was, no commitment could possibly be made at that time! I told him I truly hoped that his persuasiveness had been effective. His answer was to shrug his shoulders. "I did the best I could," he replied, with a charming, if not wholly convincing, smile.

Our hesitancy on this occasion was out of keeping with the strong conviction that our grand plan would be successful. Nevertheless, all of us chafed at the string of victories achieved over the past year in Iran by the anti-Shah, pro-Mossadegh forces and by our opposite numbers in the Soviet apparatus. Wouldn't it be nice, I thought, if we could snatch one small victory from them now, before the big one? Hence, we took great pains to investigate all "feelers" from any reasonable source. One of the feelers stands out in my mind because it emanated directly from the enemy camp—the Russian Embassy. Following it up proved exciting and somewhat dangerous for us. It was terminal—as later events made clear—for the originator.

One cold, bright afternoon in March, George announced that an East European, living in Teheran, who had been reporting to us for some time was in touch with a high Soviet diplomat. The Russian appeared to be contemplating defection. "I have told our agent," George said, "that all steps will be taken to assure the defector's safety, particularly during the trickiest stages of the operation. That will be when we must spirit the man away from the chosen meeting point to a place of sanctuary in Teheran. It is a 'safe house' you know well, Kim. From there we can whisk him out of the country."

A tobacconist's shop on Ferdowsi Square was the contact point first selected. It lay along the route of the periodic, early-evening drive taken by the diplomat and his inevitable companion, a burly, uniformed chauffeur. According to George's emigré contact, this offered the official a reasonable excuse to stop and make a purchase. The pick-up time had been set for between 6:00 and 7:00 P.M. To protect this valuable prize, arrangements from our side were carefully drawn up.

George, riding in a rather ancient black Renault driven by one of the more athletic young members of our group—we were all in our thirties—would proceed around and around Ferdowsi Square, with an occasional detour to break the monotony, throughout the appointed period. Two cars with several men in each were stationed at opposite sides of the square as support for the moment of pick-up. Contrary to normal practice, all of us were armed. Doubting that the

Russian chauffeur would be any the less prepared, we nonetheless ventured confidently forth to our posts in the square named after one of Persia's most magnificent poets. But fortune eluded us.

I recall vividly the long vigil in the back of a cramped but well-covered Land Rover and the ceaseless roundelay of the battered Renault, our eyes straining to catch the hoped-for signal. At that point the plan called for George to alert us in triumph by doffing the elegant dark homburg that was his habitual badge. Sadly, this announcement that the target had been sighted did not materialize that evening, nor the following. We tried once more and then gave it up.

We regrouped, and, two days later, our agent made contact again, establishing a location that seemed curiously and dangerously convenient: a greengrocer's open-air stall, scarcely fifty yards from the massive wrought-iron gates of the Russian Embassy. Suddenly we were asking ourselves, "Who is courting whom?" Instinct told us this would be the last chance and we prepared accordingly. In addition to the small Belgian pistol with which we all were once again equipped, I still retain a bulky black tube that constituted the tear gas "pencil" which George handed to me at the conclusion of the final briefing on that late-winter afternoon. I knew that it worked because I have tested it since then, but at the moment I had to take it on faith.

Those of us who were involved in that evening's effort were still convinced that the Russian diplomat was sincere in wishing to defect. We were equally sincere in our offer of providing sanctuary. Unfortunately success was to elude both parties.

Contact was made that evening within fifteen minutes of the time that the three cars took up their positions. Two were stationed roughly one hundred yards apart, across from the embassy's gates, on the opposite side of the street which constitutes the southern boundary of the Russian compound. I thought it an incongruous coincidence that the street's name was, and still is, Khiabane Roosevelt (not after me, to be sure, but after FDR). The third car was parked opposite the greengrocer's, which lay only fifty yards down the street directly facing the headquarters of the enemy. High walls and two-storied buildings obscured my view and that of the others who waited in the two cars on Khiabane Roosevelt. We could not see what happened in front of the fruit stand, which was only scant yards away. It did happen very quickly, but that was all the good that could be said for it. Within thirty seconds after the long black Zim rolled through the swiftly opened gates and out into the dusk, the operation was over. Stopping across from the open-air shop, the diplomat alighted on schedule and, walking over, paused beside the lone customer who stood, newspaper under one arm, surveying the abundance of carrots and beets that were the staple of every *farangi*'s (foreigner's) diet. A word, a gesture, a glance—whatever passed between the Russian and our Eastern European friend convinced the chauffeur that his passenger was about to be ours. Without hesitation, he spun the car across the quiet street, lunged toward the far door, opened it and with one long arm retrieved his charge. From the cover of the cramped Land Rover I heard the roar of the Zim's engine and seconds later saw our prize vanish beyond the somber reaches of the iron gates.

Some weeks later a new name replaced an old one near the top of the Soviet diplomatic list in Teheran. The man we had been seeking to support was reported to have died. There was a hint of suicide; we thought murder more likely.

It was not much later that the Russians sent a new Ambassador to Teheran. Their choice was Anatol

Lavrentiev, an experienced "diplomat" who had staged the Communist take-over of Czechoslovakia in 1948. We were naturally interested, though we could hardly claim to be surprised at the selection of a man with that kind of background.

I stayed on for a week after our abortive effort to pick up the Soviet defector. Discreet contact was effected with the Boscoe brothers, who indicated that, so far as they were concerned, the situation was all "go!" I also advised two of Cuvier's top assistants, Bill Herman and Dick Manville, of our intentions. This was a step I had not wished to take until I was positive that the operation would go forward. Knowing of the desires of the new Republican management in Washington, and of the impatient conviction of our British friends, I was sure that if I came back with a favorable report, everyone would wish to move as quickly as possible. Still, Cuvier was cautious. "You mustn't rush things, Kim," he kept saying. But Herman, who was to take George's place as chief area representative, and Dick Manville were both convinced that the time was ripe. So was I. The significance of Mossadegh's effort to push the Shah into exile—which is what it would have been in effect—and of the crowd's mobilization to urge him to stay seemed to us most encouraging. I left Iran full of optimism.

Word from Teheran continued to be encouraging. I had a final meeting in Beirut with Cuvier and Herman. The latter was full of cheer and confidence. "Old Mossadegh may look as though he's on top," he told me, "but the hand of the Tudeh, and behind them the Russians, is showing more openly every day. The army, and the people, *must* see it."

George was a bit more restrained, although even he was now hopeful. "It will be no shoo-in," he said. "But I do think it's possible. Essentially Bill is right about the army and the people. However, as you know, there is still one most important job to be done. The Shah remembers most unhappily the reception Mossadegh got in Washington. He will need to be convinced that the U.S. is on his side. The British too, if possible, though that is less important. But he must be sure of the U.S. And it is harder and harder to get access to H.I.M. under conditions that he and you will find satisfactory for frank talk."

Cuvier had a point. I recognized it, was bothered by it. Yet I was confident that it could be overcome.

When time came to obtain final governmental approval for the Mossadegh project, the problem on the British side was simple. Both Churchill and Eden had taken an active personal interest in the project. They had been kept advised of current progress; so when the time came for the policy decision, their blessing was already assured. However, Eden at least read the final draft of the plan very carefully, making marginal notations in his own handwriting.

On the American side, the matter was quite different. Although after my mission was completed President Eisenhower received an extensive personal briefing, I doubt very much that he had anything other than the most "broad brush" outline of what was proposed. Nor do I think that Foster Dulles gave the plan anything like the detailed, even loving, scrutiny that his British opposite number undertook.

CHAPTER

9

"Some for the Glories of this world; and some
Sigh for the Prophet's Paradise to come;
    Ah, take the Cash, and let the Credit go
Nor heed the rumble of a distant Drum."

Omar Khayyam (late 11th century)

After the final meeting in Foster Dulles' office, my departure for Teheran had been held up for some days. There was an unexpected problem. My annual physical examination—a strict Agency requirement—had come due, and the doctor had discovered a kidney stone. Getting an independent medical opinion—largely imaginary, I admit—I argued that it must have been caused by long, hot, dry rides across the desert. That was fair enough, the doctor agreed, but my further assumption that it would not, therefore, give me any problem he found laughable. While he was still laughing I got Allen Dulles to overrule him. (Allen may have lacked medical experience, but he had the proper sense of urgency.) By the time I got back from Iran the stone had moved appreciably, out of the kidney and down into the ureter. The doctor who cut it out expressed sympathy for all the pain I must have suffered. When I said I hadn't felt a thing he was amazed, probably unbelieving. The only explanation I can offer, which I said to the doctor, was that the nervous strain I was under must have lubricated my internal organs most substantially. But what I told him was absolutely true: I never had the slightest twinge of pain.*

Anyway, when I arrived in Beirut once again I spent the evening with Farid and Yolande Nashashibi. And once again I was subjected to some bland probing, though this time, since I was not flying out of Beirut, Farid could not hold up my departure.

"So you're on your way to Iran once again, Kim? I trust you are keeping yourself gainfully employed!" I could almost see the quotation marks on the last two words and the exclamation point following them. "Surely you and the British must be planning some sort of, er, *reaction* to what old Mossy has been doing." He gave me a quizzical look of inquiry.

I laughed. "Farid, you know very well that if I did have an answer to your question, I couldn't give it. We can discuss the weather in Iran, whether Demavand is

*Incidentally, the security people at the Agency were most concerned lest I say something indiscreet while coming out of anesthesia. So they assigned a special nurse, who had TOP SECRET clearance, to look after me. When, on awakening in my hospital room after it was all over, I asked her what I had said, she simply gave me a mischievous look. "Nothing that betrayed any *state* secrets," she assured me. In turn I assured her that I had no other kind.

still crowned with snow, or we can talk about something else. What do you hear from Cairo?"

Egypt, and Gamal Abdel Nasser, were of sufficient interest to Farid to keep conversation going for some while. Then Yolande and I discussed families until it was time for me to make a polite departure. When I left his home Farid gave me the traditional French hunter's send-off: *"Merde à la chasse!"*

Other words occurred to me as we drove out of Beirut the next morning. I remembered what my father wrote of his arrival in East Africa with *his* father, T.R., in 1909 on *The African Game Trails* trip. "It was a great adventure, and all the world was young!" I felt as he must have felt then. My nerves tingled, my spirits soared as we moved up the mountain road toward Damascus. This was always an exciting drive. I had made it countless times, first with a friend from our Jerusalem consulate in the spring of 1944 when the road was practically free of traffic. Now it was a very different proposition, with busses, trucks, and large American cars, many of them taxis, competing for every inch of roadway. It was not unusual to come around a curve on the four-lane mountain highway and find, racing toward you, a bus on the inner lane, a truck trying to pass the bus, a taxi trying to pass the truck and still another car trying to pass the taxi, all simultaneously. Rusting wreckage gruesomely underlined the risks of travel, but the beauty and coolness of mountains and the rich Bekaa Valley made the drive to Damascus beautiful—unlike anything between Damascus and the mountains on the Iranian frontier.

In Damascus I picked up Francis Granger, who was once again going to make the trip to Teheran with me. We had a pleasant dinner with friends and left in the comparative cool of the evening to take the pipeline road for Baghdad. You miss nothing driving that road at night—except heat and glare and long miles of rock and sand. In the early dawn we reached Rutbah, where busses and camel caravans alike rested and watered. Thence we pressed on for Baghdad, driving at first sunlight through a Bedouin tribe on the move. Camels, goats, donkeys and small children were strung out for miles. Soon the full force of the day reached us. The sky was a pale steel gray, paler than gun metal, and the sun came blisteringly hot off the sand. When we stopped to drink beer in the meager shade of the car, sweat appeared on our arms as fast as we swallowed.

We rested for half a day and a night in Baghdad, staying with another old friend and keeping discreetly out of sight. Now that we were drawing close to the scene of action, our desire was to keep my arrival in Iran as secret as possible. The State Department had an unyielding policy against the issuance of false passports or, indeed, their use by official or unofficial personnel under any circumstances. Private citizens, of course, would be prosecuted for such use. I could easily have equipped myself with one—say, in Rome, where American passports were available for a relatively modest sum. But I did not feel it really necessary. Surely we could enter quite securely by car through Khanequin and the Iraq–Iran frontier. While airport records were comparatively easy to keep and were readily accessible to curious officials, it would be months, if not years, before all the border records reached a central point where they could be consulted and collated.

As it turned out, on July 19, 1953, we encountered an unusually listless, stupid and semiliterate immigration-customs fellow at Khanequin. In those days U.S. passports carried, as they do not now, some brief description of any notable features of the holder. With encouragement and help from me, the guard laboriously transcribed my name as "Mr. Scar on Right Forehead." This I found a good omen.*

We had left Baghdad well before dawn so were able to lunch in Hamadan and reach Teheran before our embassy closed. The trip was uneventful; we arrived hot and dusty. There was no reason to linger at the embassy—in fact, I did not even enter it—our only purpose being to find Bill Herman, newly named senior area representative, to get him to lead us to his house in the mountains. This was very close to where I had stayed with the Reynoldses the previous year, on a *koochi* (lane) just below the village not far off the old Shimran Road, in a walled compound with fruit and shade trees. It boasted a small, very welcome swimming pool. The residence combined suitable discretion with accessibility. Bill, his wife Jane, their two children and I were to share the pool and the house for most of the next six weeks. Bill I was already fond of. Over the next weeks I grew to love his family with the affection that grows from sharing a special kind of experience. We lived in a world of our own, much of the time cut off from the outside, yet being at some moments most intensely, most *actively*, caught up in it. The house became home. I was able to lie by their pool and sun myself between necessary ventures outside the walls for the various meetings I had to attend. I have rarely felt so completely at ease, and I resented it when the pressure of events and security requirements made it advisable for me to move down into our own agency compound during the critical phase of the

*See de Villiers, p. 176. "On July 6[*sic*], 1953, a tanned, thirty-seven-year-old American presented himself to the customs officer at Qaar-E-Shirin on the border between Iraq and Iran." The author says A.W.D. sent me to "get rid of Mossadegh." I am further described as the son of T.R. Also, on p. 177, he says the border inspector wrote "scar on left cheek" where he should have written my name. Well intended by de Villiers but once again inaccurate. He does give my age correctly—which should have led him to question whether I was really likely to be my grandfather's son. T.R. was past sixty when he died in January 1919, and I was not yet three years old.

operation. I lost then the splendid isolation that gave me not only detachment but confidence. But by then excitement had overwhelmed us. Nitty-gritty details rolled off the rhinoceros hide created by total involvement.

Before Francis left, just twenty-four hours after his arrival, I heard him regaling the Herman children with an imaginative account of our trip.

"It was truly weird, crossing the desert at night and then encountering these strange supernatural beasts at dawn. They were giant shaggy creatures carrying what I believe must have been little monkeys hidden under baskets on their backs, so the baskets wiggled as they walked."

"Oh," said young William, suddenly enlightened. "You mean *camels*. We have them here. But those aren't monkeys in baskets on their backs," he added scornfully. "Those are humps. Haven't you ever seen a camel?"

Francis shook his head in puzzlement. "Never seen anything like that before in my whole life. Camels, you say? Well, they're queer beasts, I can testify to that.

"Then when we arrived at the border to Iran, there was a very strange character in the guardpost. He insisted on examining the head of your Uncle Kim—" I had already achieved the status of uncle—"and finally he said, 'Hello, Mr. Scar on Right Forehead.' What *do* you think he could have meant?"

This time he had the children properly mystified. Triumphantly, he was waving his arms and cackling like a chicken—don't ask why—as he took off on his return to Beirut.

The first few days in Teheran were spent catching up on the reports from Washington and being briefed by George Cuvier, Bill and other members of our local staff. Things were moving along steadily. Tempo in the anti-Mossadegh press was increasing gradually, and the anti-Shah, anti-American press was becoming ever more frantic and vehement. Tension was rising. Half a dozen times a day at Bill's and other American residences the telephone would ring and whoever answered it would hear nothing but heavy, hostile breathing or shrill epithets. The children rapidly got used to this. They entertained themselves by trying to cap each other's experiences and the obscene language to which they had been exposed. Orders had gone out for General Zahedi's arrest, but he was in safe hiding. At that particular moment he was in the mountains only five miles or so from our compound. My idea was to get in touch with him through his son, Ardeshir, a friend of mine. However, George Cuvier thought otherwise. He arranged a meeting for me with another Iranian well equipped to serve as our contact with General Zahedi.

"Dick Manville knows a good friend of Zahedi's, a chap named Mustapha Vaysi. He is, you could say, 'notorious' for being pro-American. And he's a gutsy young man. At the moment Mossadegh's minions, his police and security people, have been leaving Mustapha pretty much alone. At least for the time being. Just a few months ago he was badly beaten up by them. But I think it would be safe for Dick to bring him to say goodbye to me, and you could see him then."

Dick Manville was the "case officer" George had selected to be the principal contact with Mustapha. They were about the same age, in their mid-twenties. He had attended the American University of Beirut after his primary education in Teheran and Isfahan. Then he took a degree in Agricultural Engineering from Texas A & M, graduating in 1950. Naturally he spoke English, though there was a strong Persian cast to it. Texas had a special interest in Persian students because one of its senior professors had spent some years in Iran, and there were many Persians in the university. In any case, Dick was fluent in Farsi, which was a great advantage.

Thus it was that Dick brought Mustapha Vaysi to George's farewell reception, which took place at George's house just three days after my arrival. It seemed an appropriate moment, as safe as any opportunity for direct contact could be. Discretion prevented me from attending the party in person, but I did go to George's house early to closet myself in an upstairs bedroom. There, during the noisy peak of the revelry below, Dick brought Mustapha to see me.

We greeted each other warmly, although we had never met before. Naturally Mustapha wanted to take me to see his friend the general immediately.

"Zahedi is not too far away. I'm sure Dick has told you. He is up in the mountains not far behind his own house—a few miles from here." His eyes gleamed with excitement. "You *must* come. He'll be so anxious to see you."

It was hard to resist his enthusiasm, but I felt I had to.

"Naturally I want to meet General Zahedi as soon as possible. I've heard so much about him I feel I know him already. But you must understand how careful I have to be." Dick, under the misapprehension that Mustapha already knew me, had told him my real name. "Only you, General Zahedi, and His Imperial Majesty will know my real name. To the rest of the world I am James Lochridge and hope to remain so as long as possible. That means I must see as few people as I can and *no one*, except the Shah himself, whom I've ever met before. So, much as I look forward to making the general's acquaintance, let's wait until the time is right and we can be sure that the meeting will be entirely secure."

Mustapha looked a bit disappointed, but he accepted my decision gracefully. As it turned out, I was to enjoy rather more of General Zahedi's company than I had anticipated. Meanwhile, full of hope and exuding confidence, young Vaysi left me, having arranged that we keep in touch through his friend in our local "station."

Since our operation there has, naturally, been a lot of speculation about CIA *and* Soviet agents in Iran. One British writer cheerfully translated speculation into hard fact. He found Teheran so full of U.S./ U.S.S.R. agents "that a local wit once suggested that they ought to share apartments so as to save themselves time and money in keeping one another under surveillance."* In addition to the U.S. military mission which Mossadegh, not yet wanting to break with the United States, had been unwilling to expel, "there were also some strange Americans named Jake and Red and Uncle Ami (their real names must remain secret**) who put in regular appearances around the cabarets and bars; they spoke the purest Bronx, Brooklynese or Panhandle drawls but turned out to possess an even more fluent command of Kurdish or the dialects of Kermansheh, Khorramshahr and Azerbaijan, learned at the knees of their immigrant parents. They came in to report and quench their thirst for whisky and female company, and then disappeared again for weeks on end."*** .

When you compare this horde of motley types with Bill Herman, Dick Manville, myself and the two junior officers who helped with the paperwork but made no contacts themselves, a certain air of unreality does make itself felt. Even when you include the Iranians with whom we were working closely—Nossey and

---

*Leonard Mosley, *Power Play,* Baltimore: Penquin Books, 1974, p. 213.
**A convincing bit of arrogance!
***Mosley, *op. cit.,* p. 214.

Cafron, the Boscoe brothers, Mustapha Vaysi and, in the last phase, a most helpful chap I had not yet met, Mohsen Tahuyi—we were not overcrowding the city. If you look at the Russians, they had of course the whole of the Tudeh party at their disposal. This was a far larger group than the Boscoe brothers' allies, unless you count almost the whole army, the police and the people—the general public—who we hoped would throng to H.I.M.'s support. But I doubt whether the Russians had any more of their own case officers, or any more Iranian "principal agents," than we did.

One avenue of approach was considered early in our deliberations. Before I had even reached Teheran we had already made an important effort to start things moving, to satisfy the Shah that the West was not opposed but ready to support him. Britisher Gordon Somerset had become acquainted with H.I.M.'s twin sister, Princess Ashraf, while serving in her country. Mossadegh had mounted such a press campaign against her that it seemed best for her to leave Iran and she had gone to Switzerland. Gordon had proposed that he and one of our people approach her there, inform her of the American/British determination to support her brother and prevail on her to return to Teheran to advise her brother of this decision.

We selected Charles Mason, a major who had been loaned to us by the U.S. Air Force with the idea that he would be assigned to Teheran after—and if—AJAX was successful. Charles, who regarded himself as *the* lady-killer of the twentieth century, accepted the assignment with enthusiasm. He was completely bowled over by the attractive princess—which may well have been the reason why, when he arrived in Iran after the event, he proved to be so indiscreetly talkative that we had to recall him. As it was, during the Swiss meeting, he would barely let Gordon squeeze a word in edgewise. When he could, Gordon spoke to good effect.

"Princess," he explained, "the British and the Americans wish to help your brother the Shahanshah put this upstart Mossadegh in his proper place." Gordon, with some Scottish blood in him, *always* referred to the British ahead of the Americans and referred to Premier Mossadegh as though he were an unruly lower-school boy. But Mason was already talking again as soon as he had got the essential words out.

A woman of exceptional courage, the princess responded enthusiastically to their proposal. "Of course I'll go to talk to my brother immediately! How soon can you get me on an airplane?" It made no difference to her that Mossadegh had been, most expressly and expressively, hostile to her. Within thirty-six hours she was on her way to Teheran.

But her arrival in early July was criticized bitterly in the government-controlled press. Accordingly, when she did meet with H.I.M., they were both wary and suspicious that, somehow or other, they might be under surveillance. Frank talk seemed to both of them most risky. They spoke, therefore, in guarded platitudes. It was not a satisfactory discussion. Subject to all the pressures that the Tudeh and the Prime Minister could muster against her, Princess Ashraf returned to Switzerland, alarmed and disappointed.*

So the attempt to communicate with H.I.M. through his sister had to be written off as a failure. One more effort lay within the allowed boundaries. If that failed, and it looked as if it well might fail, then I would have to fall back on my own resources, forbidden at the moment though they might be.

---

*Mosley, *op. cit.*, pp. 414–15, quite inaccurately reports Allen Dulles' meeting with Loy Henderson and Princess Ashraf in Switzerland. Henderson was never there during this period, and the princess certainly never met Allen there or anywhere else at this time. In later years they may well have encountered each other, though I do not know where or when.

The messenger remaining available was General H. Norman Schwarzkopf, the man who had commanded the Imperial Iranian Gendarmerie from 1942 until 1948. Now the general was ostensibly, almost ostentatiously, on a round-the-world tour. His stopover in Teheran was meant to appear just a casual one, for old time's sake, to visit friends he had not seen for many years. But, needless to say, neither Mossadegh nor the Tudeh/Communist press chose to regard it as such. The propaganda blasts against his presence at this time in this place made any meaningful discussion between him and the Shah close to impossible. He did ask for an audience and one was granted him. When he finally went to the palace, however, the Shah would not talk inside, fearing that the chambers were "bugged." The two of them, alone in the garden but still most uneasy, had a nerve-racking, inconclusive conversation.

H.I.M. was courteous but, naturally, cautious. He was, he told Schwarzkopf, most grateful for the confidence the United States government was showing in him. He appreciated their generous offers of support. But the situation was, as his visitor could certainly appreciate, most difficult, most delicate. The last thing he as Shah wanted was to promote a destructive civil war. He did not exactly quote one of my favorite American ambassadors (Jefferson Caffery, then on his last post in Cairo), who was always cabling Washington, when pestered about the local situation, that he was going to "play it by ear." But that was the substance of his message.

There are of course many wild tales of General Schwarzkopf's activities. According to Leonard Mosley—who does tell a good story—the general arrived "armed with a diplomatic passport and a couple of large bags." These latter contained "millions of dollars." He supposedly called on General Hassan

Arfa, whom Mosley describes as being "diplomatical-ly" ill on his estate near Teheran; on General Zahedi, "also in hiding on his estate"; and on H.I.M. Only the latter call actually took place. Here and subsequently it appears that Mosley is relying on General Arfa's book, *Under Five Shahs* (London: John Murray, 1964). According to Arfa, Mossadegh reacted to Schwarzkopf's visits—as he did in fact react to his only visit, which was to the Shah—by abolishing the Majlis, "'a nest of thieves,' declaring a referendum, and asking by referendum for the power to deal with other brainless agents of international reaction." He made it quite clear that the latter phrase was intended as a reference to the Shah. The popular vote did produce "fights at the polls" but very few votes against Mossadegh. "In truth, the old man in pyjamas did not need to manipulate the referendum, for"—Mosley believes—"the masses were with him, even if the army, police, and landowners were not."* The "fights" did indeed, as they were intended to, intimidate many voters. And, of course, the army was still obeying General Riahi's orders, seeing as yet no reason not to. When the conflict between H.I.M. and Mossadegh with his Tudeh–Soviet supporters became unmistak-ably clear, the "masses" *and* "army, police, and land-owners" rallied strongly to the Shah.

In any event, Schwarzkopf came to report to me at Herman's house before leaving Iran to continue his tour. He was a bluff, hearty man who made his concern unmistakably plain.

"Kim," he told me sadly, seriously, "you simply are not going to be able to deal with the Shahanshah through *any* intermediary. Arrangements can't be made that way. Of course they can't be made openly

Ibid., pp. 216, 219.

either—for all the world to watch. You know damn well our enemies would be the first to see and the first to act.

"Somehow or other I'm convinced that you will have to meet with H.I.M. personally. You've told me that your bosses back home are worried that if you meet H.I.M. your identity will become public knowledge and they don't want that. On the other hand, if you confer with H.I.M. face to face, it will certainly establish your credentials beyond any doubt. And if this undertaking fails—"he gave me such a comically gloomy look that I almost laughed—"we'll all be in such hot soup that I don't really think disclosure of your name could make much difference."

I nodded. "General, I couldn't agree more. For the most part I can continue to work anonymously—here from Bill's house or discreetly from a small cubbyhole next to Bill's office. But somehow or other I'm going to have to get together with the Shah. He'll have to have a remarkable memory to remember me—after all, we met but once about six years ago—but I understand that's just what he does have. And I agree with you if he does recall me, that wouldn't be too bad. If nothing worse than that happens, we'll be in good shape!"

If Schwarzkopf had been fluent in French, he might well have repeated Farid Nashashibi's farewell: *"Merde à la chasse!"* In any case, he clearly shared the sentiment as he departed. And, in a strange way, I felt satisfied. I had been sure from the beginning that a personal meeting would be necessary. Securely and alone, the Shah and I could resolve the many difficult problems confronting us. This could only be done on a person-to-person basis. In all likelihood we would have to meet not once but several times. So the sooner we got to it, the better.

"Go tell court-huntsmen that the king will ride."
John Donne (d. 1631)

During the two weeks after my arrival, the pace of events in Iran had accelerated sharply. Donald Wilber, the most reliable historian on post-World War II happenings, wrote of Mossadegh's position at the opening of this vital period:

> By this time he was no longer regarded by foreign correspondents as a curious figure—a pyjama-clad weeper—but as a master in gauging and directing public opinion. Within several of the social strata his popularity remained high, but many of the most influential followers had fallen away because he had offended them or failed to deliver anticipated rewards for this support. Exercising his plenary powers Mossadegh had resorted to a number

of types of control: extension of martial law; appointment of military commanders personally loyal to him; . . . suspension of the Senate; suspension of elections for the *Majlis*: . . . this activity seemed contrary to the nature of the men who had long insisted that elections must be completely free and had sternly opposed the imposition of martial law and of restrictive press laws. On the other hand, the National Front regarded Mossadegh as the emotional symbol of a regenerated Iran. . . . By sweeping the British—oil company, diplomats, and businessmen— from Iran, Mossadegh engendered a spirit of national self-confidence, long lacking in Iran.[*]

By the end of July many elements had withdrawn from the National Front. Among them were the Toilers' party, led by Dr. Mozaffar Baghai; Hussein Makki, who had made himself "the hero of nationalization" by turning off the valve to stop the flow of oil at Abadan; the rightist Sumka and Pan-Iranist parties; and many of the mullahs, including Kashani—all had turned against Mossadegh. Despite strict controls more and more of the press was no longer supporting the National Front but was, at least cautiously and obliquely, critical. Within the Majlis attacks on the government grew in frequency. The merchants were worried, their worry reflected in a drop in the rial (the national currency) from 75 to the dollar in 1951 to a July low of 130.

Mossadegh reacted by attempting to convince the public that the United States was behind him. At the same time he was warning Washington that unless financial aid was forthcoming Iran would turn Communist. More and more he made himself seem the only voice of the "national movement." Having rid himself of the Senate, he went to work upon the Majlis. First all the members of the National Front resigned,

---

[*]Wilber, *op. cit.*, pp. 120–21.

making a quorum impossible. Then, on July 25, he decreed a referendum to determine whether the present Majlis should be retained or dissolved. Voting was in conspicuously separate booths, closely watched, with voters showing anti-government inclinations severely intimidated. This was reflected in the results: over two million for dissolution, only one thousand two hundred for retention. But he was left with a problem. "Free" elections might be swept by the Tudeh, who could carry him further than he wanted to go.

Fortunately—for us if not precisely for him—this was a possibility he did not have to face. Before the elections could take place, our own preparations had matured. Action, marred by bad luck in the beginning but rewarded for persistence at the end, was shortly to begin.

Before General Schwarzkopf's arrival from Teheran, Bill Herman and I had already established contact with the principal representatives of British Intelligence, Nossey and Cafron. It was agreed that the two of us should handle all dealings with them. Bill arranged for an evening rendezvous at their chosen site that was within a mile and a half of Bill's house. I was introduced to them as Mr. James Lochridge, the name under which they were to know me for over a year. (Very soon they were calling me Jim.) There were many Persians unconnected with our operations who knew me personally, but I managed to avoid seeing them. The only three Persians who knew of my connection with the operation and my true identity were the Shah, General Zahedi and Mustapha Vaysi. They were scrupulous in protecting my anonymity. There were others, the Qashqai against whom George Cuvier had warned me, who, for some reason never explained to my satisfaction, suspected my presence. Violently anti-Shah, they sent threatening messages which were intended to, and did, reach me.

Though they came to Teheran while I was there, I was able to keep out of their sight.

The setting which Nossey and Cafron had chosen for our rendezvous had a suitably conspiratorial air. It was an uninhabited house just off the main road which now runs to the Teheran Hilton Hotel. The house was big and empty, in a large compound. We rarely went inside but sat in the garden under one bare electric light bulb, around a wooden table with uneven legs on chairs that were equally dilapidated. The heavy gate of the compound was opened when our headlights blinked on it and closed immediately after us. Darkness encircled our table except for the occasional patch of moonlight that was able to get through the thick foliage of the trees above us. To liven the gloom of our surroundings, our two allies brought various amenities—plates of sliced cucumber, pistachio nuts and other delicacies from their own homes and, without fail, a thermos of ice, glasses for each person and a bottle of Johnnie Walker Scotch. Despite the surroundings, our meetings were always lively affairs. The younger of the two, whom we nicknamed "Laughing Boy," jabbered away in Persian. We knew the elder as the "Mad Musician"; he talked equally constantly in English, sometimes interpreting, sometimes ignoring what his associate was saying. The reason for his sobriquet was his addiction to the piano, basically to what was then known as the "player piano." This had a place over the keyboard into which could be inserted a perforated roll of paper; start it rolling, and it played. The "Mad Musician" sat on the piano stool and moved his fingers more or less in accord with the keys. All his rolls were waltzes, mostly by father or son Johann Strauss. Every now and then, to vary our routine, Bill and I would refer to him as the "Waltz King."

In the meantime I was entertaining myself in a mildly dangerous way by playing tennis, either at the

Turkish Embassy court or on those of the French Institute. I played with a girl in the U.S. Embassy staff against one of our own officers and his wife. The danger came not from the game but from a habit I had then, and still have, of saying, "Oh, *Roosevelt*" when I missed a shot. I did my best to pass myself off as a blackhearted reactionary Republican to whom "Roosevelt," meaning FDR, was a heartfelt obscenity.

With Nossey and Cafron I was dealing primarily in terms of the Shah and the problem of communications with him. Now that the time had come when it was necessary that I see H.I.M. myself, I consulted them as to how I should make the approach. The answer was not difficult. They, too, had discerned that, unknowingly, British Intelligence and the CIA shared an agent—we called him "Rosenkrantz"—who had ready access to the Shahanshah. So "Laughing Boy," who was closer to him, arranged that he advise H.I.M.—and him only—that an American authorized to speak for Eisenhower *and* Churchill desired a secret audience. He had, the agent was instructed to say, an important personal message from the two of them.

As "Mad Musician" translated what his associate would put to our intermediary, it did not sound too appropriate. "Little Shot from the U.S. has lively word from the two Big Shots in America and England. Word is, 'Pull up your socks and let's get going!'" Our Persian allies dissolved in laughter. Bill and I did not find it all that funny.

"Just make sure the substance gets through unmistakably clear," said Bill, forcefully if somewhat ungrammatically. "There must be no foul-up on this exchange. If we don't get Mr. Lochridge through to H.I.M. on this exchange we probably never will."

I added my own words of warning, but nothing we said made any dent on our allies' hilarity. We were becoming used to it, and we realized that it did not indicate any lack of serious intent on their part. But it was unnerving. The last thing we needed at that moment was to be unnerved.

However, their confidence was justified, if hilarity was not. Their emissary reported back that the Shah had received my message thoughtfully but positively.

"A car from the palace—but not an official-looking car—will pick you up at midnight tonight just outside our garden," said the musician Cafron, with only a faint giggle. It was not, of course, "their" garden, but that didn't seem worthwhile to argue just then. "We will wait here with Bill and celebrate on your return."

I could only wish I felt as confident as the "Mad Musician" that we would have something to celebrate. We were already in the garden, though it was only just after ten. Two hours to wait! I considered my costume. If not appropriate for a royal audience, it did seem good for these rather peculiar circumstances. I had on a dark turtleneck shirt, Oxford-gray slacks and a pair of black-topped *givehs,* rope-soled cloth-covered Persian footwear somewhere between shoes and bedroom slippers. Not exactly smart but suitably unobtrusive. So we sat around nervously, N. and C. jabbering as usual, for the next two hours. I didn't dare have a drink, but the others made up for my abstinence.

It was Saturday, the first of August, about to become Sunday the second. At a few minutes before midnight I walked through the long garden, escorted by Bill carrying a flashlight. We opened the gate, and I went out alone. A car was already there, waiting. It was a nondescript black sedan. The driver was obtrusively incurious and didn't say a word. Thinking the vehicle was suitably nonroyal, I got into the back seat. There was a blanket on the seat. As we approached the palace gates, I huddled down on the floor and pulled the blanket over me. But there was no need for extra caution. The sentry on duty silently, matter-of-factly, motioned us through.

Halfway between the gates and the palace steps, we halted on the driveway. A slim figure walked down the steps, along the drive, and, as the driver left, opened the door and got in beside me in the back seat. I pulled the blanket out of the way and moved over to provide room. There was enough light for us to see each other. I had no problem recognizing the finely drawn, distinctively regal features. And I was not really surprised that H.I.M. in turn recognized me immediately. (His memory for names, faces, facts and figures is truly remarkable, as I did already know.) After his first quick look, the Shah held out his hand.

"Good evening, Mr. Roosevelt. I cannot say that I expected to see you, but this is a pleasure."

"Good evening, Your Majesty. It is a long time since we met each other, and I am glad you recognize me. It may make establishing my credentials a bit easier."

H.I.M. laughed. "That will hardly be necessary. Your name and presence is all the guarantee I need."

However, I did have much to explain. First of all was my situation, how I entered Iran described as "Mr. Scar on Right Forehead." I was to be known to Nossey/Cafron and any others I had to meet—barring two—as James Lochridge. The two I was excepting were Zahedi and his admiring young friend, Mustapha Vaysi. Zahedi, as I understood it, was the Shah's choice to succeed Mossadegh as Prime Minister.

But the most important point I had to make was that I was there representing U.S. President Eisenhower and British Prime Minister Churchill.

"President Eisenhower will confirm this himself by a phrase in a speech he is about to deliver in San Francisco—actually within the next twenty-four hours. Prime Minister Churchill has arranged to have a specific change made in the time announcement on the BBC broadcast tomorrow night. Instead of saying 'It is now midnight,' the announcer will say, 'It is now'—pause—'*exactly* midnight.'"

The Shah pointed out that, having recognized me, he needed no such confirmation. However, we both agreed that it was best to establish the record clearly, with commitment on all sides.

There was not the tension, the pressure that I had expected to feel at this first meeting. The Shah was calm and collected. His matter-of-fact, thoroughly cordial attitude relaxed me also. When he had approached the car I could feel my heart pounding. Now the beat was even, my breathing regular. It was like a meeting of friends to talk over a common undertaking—but one on which neither of them expected any difficulty in agreeing. I was under the impression that time had been passing with remarkable speed, that dawn must be about to break. Apparently H.I.M. shared this feeling. So after the briefest review by each of us of the situation as he saw it, we agreed to meet the following night. Same time, same place.

"Good night—or should I say good morning?—Mr. Roosevelt. I am glad to welcome you once again to my country."

"And I am very glad to be here, Your Majesty. I am full of confidence that our undertaking will succeed." I felt the words a little stilted, but I also felt that it might be *lèse-majesté* for me to repeat Farid's hunter's farewell, *"Merde à la chasse!"*

So we parted, cordial but still a bit formal. (The formality would not last for long.) The Shah got out of the car, recalled the driver, and I was returned to the garden from which I had come.

"Back at the ranch" I was greeted with hilarity enhanced by the liquid refreshment which Bill Herman and our Iranian allies had been consuming in my absence. But my spirits were every bit as high as theirs. Dawn did not come as soon as I had expected, but we toasted it exuberantly when it finally arrived.

On the next night the driver picked me up as before and we—H.I.M. and I—took up the discussion where we had left off.

"I take it that your principals—" the Shah smiled faintly as he chose this word—"agree with my choice of Fazlollah Zahedi to replace Mossadegh as Prime Minister."

"That is correct, sir. The British were not too happy at first. They remember that they thought it necessary to arrest him in Isfahan during World War Two and to hold him under arrest in Palestine until after peace was concluded."

"I remember that too," said the Shah dryly. "The officer who seized him was Colonel Fitzroy Maclean. He has written a book about his travels though the Soviet Union and later served—with Mihajlovic? No, with Tito—in Yugoslavia."

"You're quite right." I found saying "Your Majesty" or even "Sir" every time I addressed the Shahanshah a bit tiresome, even redundant. I tried to do it every five or six sentences, which seemed to cause no offense.

"I'm afraid I get his book mixed up with a couple by Peter Fleming, who made a trip through some of the same country at about the same time. Three books— *News from Tartary, A Forgotten Journey,* and *Escape to Adventure;* I think the last one is Maclean's."

The Shah shrugged his shoulders. "We have more important matters to discuss right now." He was right and I colored with embarrassment. But a smile made it clear he meant no reproof.

The "important matters" covered a great deal of ground. We had agreed on Zahedi as the replacement for Mossadegh, and we further agreed that the general would choose his own cabinet. H.I.M. had profound distrust of certain officers, beginning with the "Commander in Chief,"* as Mossadegh styled General Taqi Riahi, although according to the constitution the Shah was supreme commander of all Iranian forces. There were other officers he named who he was certain were committed to Mossadegh and Riahi. But the great bulk of the army—officers, noncoms and enlisted men— were, in the Shah's judgment, completely loyal.

Our assessment, I told H.I.M., was precisely the same as his. Events were to prove us both correct.

Another vital question concerned timing. As an American, naturally I was all for speed. Americans believe that the more quickly we move, the safer we are. The Persians, including their Shahanshah, have the patience of millennia behind them. They are *not* inclined to rush things. Sometimes I call the delay procrastination. But the Shah quite rightly pointed out that we had many decisions to make and to agree upon between us. Impressed, I was also relieved to find him not only perceptive but actually emphasizing the importance of joint conclusion. Here was no insistence on a royal prerogative; I was accepted as the representative of American and British interests and treated as such.

One priority—just a precaution, it seemed to me at the time—was to agree on what course the Shah should follow in case of difficulty, betrayal or whatever, in Teheran. Now that it was clear that we could not act immediately, every passing day represented increasing danger. Our calculations might go awry. Preparations, inescapably necessary, added to the risks of exposure. We were both reluctant to admit these risks. But we were both aware also of the necessity for decision on a joint course of action should things go wrong.

*His title more properly was "Chief of the Army's General Staff."

"We *must* make some plans," the Shah told me.

I had to agree. "There should not be any real danger. But Your Majesty is right. We have to plan as though there could be."

When he came to propose the course he might follow, I was somewhat unnerved.

"I think I should go to Shiraz. It is far enough from Teheran, yet easily accessible. It would give me the maneuverability I should have. Don't you think so?"

"From a geographical point of view, sir, it certainly makes sense. My only worry is the Qashqai tribe. Shiraz is their headquarters. I don't think we can trust them one inch. Going there, you might well fall into their hands, and who knows what they would do?" I thought I knew very well, *too* well. H.I.M. would get short shrift indeed. I entirely shared George Cuvier's visceral estimate of their intent. They were bitter enemies of the crown. Vengeful hostility was all that could be expected of them. Implacable, they would say, rather than treacherous. Personally, I would combine the traits and call them "implacably treacherous." Naturally I did not get so specific with the Shah. But later happenings were to prove my judgment correct.

Meanwhile the Shah was nodding, accepting the estimate despite its unpalatability.

"Isfahan is also a Qashqai center. So what else? We can't think of Meshed. It is too far away and too close to the Soviets—closer to them by far than it is to Teheran."

"What about Tabriz?" I asked. "We hear encouraging reports that it is already anti-Mossadegh and we believe that at the first sign of confrontation between a deposed Prime Minister and you, the unquestioned chief of state, Tabrizi would rush to your support *en masse*."

He smiled. "I feel sure that you are right. But the

danger is that they are directly under the Russian gun, the logical line of attack if the U.S.S.R. should decide to move against me."

Once again, I had to agree. Tabriz did not seem to be the ideal retreat. The Shah gave the matter further thought.

"This reminds me, as a good Moslem, of Mohammed's Hegira in 622 A.D. by your calendar, year one by ours. He 'fled' purely to dramatize his situation. I could do the same.

"Really," he concluded, "I think this is what I'll do. Once we've made the final arrangements, and I have signed the *firmans* [royal decrees], dismissing Mossadegh and appointing Zahedi, I'll fly up to the Caspian. If by any horrible chance things go wrong, the Empress and I"—this was the first mention either of us had made of Queen Soraya—"will take our plane straight to Baghdad. From there we can look the situation over and decide to what place we should return."

Without further discussion, this became the plan. Neither of us really thought it would be necessary, and neither of us mentioned it again. One thing did happen that made me nervous. Evidently the police had been tipped off that something mysterious was going on at the villa where Bill and I were meeting with Nossey and Cafron. A servant they had left behind to keep an eye on the garden reported that in mid-afternoon, when any reasonable Persian would be having a siesta, there had been a surprise raid. The gates were forced open. Cars swept in, disgorging armed men who made a very thorough search of the house and grounds. The servant was, of course, discovered and questioned. But he was able to convince the raiders that he knew nothing of any clandestine meetings. The owners— totally innocent friends of Nossey and Cafron named Rashidi—had, he said, left Teheran for the Caspian on the previous afternoon. Other than that, he had nothing to tell them. Although his interrogators were far from satisfied, they did not suspect him. But when they withdrew, he was certain they left watchers behind to keep an eye on the neighborhood.

Naturally we abandoned our garden rendezvous immediately. Thereafter we met most cautiously. Bill dropped out of contact with Nossey and Cafron entirely. The two of them provided me with a Hillman Minx taxi and a card to place in its windshield which said in Persian "ON CALL." At an agreed time I would leave the cab inconspicuously parked just off Gohack Street, not too far from the unoccupied British Ambassador's residence. Then, in my usual nondescript costume—perhaps khaki trousers, dark-blue shirt and *givehs*—I would walk out in the country to the prescribed meeting place. Soon, out of a cloud of dust, the sleek Chrysler or Buick of the day would emerge, driven usually by "Laughing Boy." We would careen wildly around through the hills conferring on developments. After what would seem to me an inexplicable amount of maniacal laughs—both allies continued to find everything inordinately funny—they would drop me off reasonably close to my Hillman Minx. In a roundabout way I would return to the Herman household.

This development I recounted to the Shah. He shrugged his shoulders and gave me a questioning look. All I could do was shrug in reply.

In the meantime we continued to explore four lines of attack that had been planned. But first, to help us keep our calm, I explained one of the security practices we followed.

"Your Majesty, I don't see any way that our conversations could be 'bugged' in this car. You were right to suspect that it would be dangerous to talk to Princess Ashraf or General Schwarzkopf in the palace, or even perhaps near any tree in your garden; but this isn't even your car. Surely old Mossy or his sidekick Riahi can't 'bug' every vehicle in Teheran."

The Shah, with a thin smile, nodded grim concurrence.

"There is one routine precaution we are taking. Everyone involved is assigned what we call a 'cryptonym' and also, for general conversational use, usually a nickname. For example, I've told you Nossey/Caffron know me as James Lochridge, but that is, I guess you'd call it, an 'alias.' I have also a pseudonym, Steven P. Mason. That is a complication you don't have to bother with. My cryptonym is RNMAKER. Yours is KGSAVOY. Your nickname, which I hope won't offend you, is 'Boy Scout.'" I got another thin smile.

"There's no need to bother you with other cryptonyms. But you might be amused by some of the nicknames. The P.M. is 'the old bugger.' General Riahi is 'smart ass.' One of the officers we're dealing with and hope to find useful is French-trained, sort of dandified and supercilious. He is 'the dancing master.' A bunch of junior officers we refer to as 'the Young Turks.' That's about it."

I returned to the "four lines of attack" which we were to explore.

"The first would be an alliance with the mullahs. We've had a lot of discussion about them. The British think they might be helpful, willing to work with us. But our principal Iranian 'allies,' whose names I will not give you—their pseudonyms are Boscoe One and Two—have always been reluctant to rely on them. Truly, I have not yet decided. We will keep sounding them out. So far all we got from them are demands for huge sums of money. And I'm not going to rely on *anyone* who will cooperate only for pay. We want patriots, not mercenaries."

The Shah nodded decisively. "I completely agree. Any loyal Iranian will help because he feels he absolutely must, because his heart tells him to. We don't need any other kind of 'ally.'"

"No, sir, we do not!" The "sir" was emphasis, not a form of address. We had been studying the mullahs with some skepticism ever since Harriman and Walters had their unsatisfactory meeting with Kashani. At that time the mullahs were supporting Mossadegh. Now, as Russian backing of the Tudeh and Tudeh backing of the ancient doctor became ever more obvious, the religious gentry had withdrawn into their shells like tortoises. I had not entirely given up hope that they might be useful allies, but I was increasingly skeptical. It looked as though my Iranian friends might be better judges than the British. Looking back today, I hope they felt infuriated and frustrated when they saw what happened on 28 Mordad, the day of reckoning. In the several days before, of course, they would have felt proven right—which would make the disappointment even greater.

"O.K. That covers the first line of attack. The second is your military support. We are agreed that except for General Riahi and a few officers very close to him, the armed forces are devotedly loyal to you. I brought a chap with me to handle the contacts with a small, carefully chosen group of officers. Your Majesty would be intrigued and amused by my man." I described Peter Stoneman in some detail, without naming him.

"He's a huge fellow, very bright, very hard-working, very determined, absolutely without humor—and as obstinate as anyone can possibly be. Of course he's a dedicated enthusiast. There's nothing more I can say, is there? He gets so carried away by his own plans, his own contacts that he can't pay attention to anything else. The other day he came to report to me. I keep away from the embassy and so does he, so we met at a friend's house in Shimran. My idea was to give him a lecture that he couldn't possibly ignore.

"So I tried. After a while it was too clear that I was not getting through. He had that glazed look in his eyes, his regular response to any argument he did not wish to hear. I stood up so that I could be sure of reaching my target—" the Shah grinned—"and kicked him sharply on the shin. This did get his attention. While I had it, I said, 'You listen to what I'm saying and act as I tell you to. Otherwise, I will personally throw you the hell out of this country.'

"Sir, that glaze vanished from his eyes, a certain respectful semicontrite look came into them, and by God he's paid attention to everything I've told him since. So far, anyhow. I'd better knock wood!" There was no wood evident in the car, so I rapped my knuckles against my forehead. This childish American gesture was new to the Shah, and he laughed—not all that heartily, but it was the first time he'd done so since I met him. Somehow I was immensely cheered.

"Anyhow, Your Majesty, with Stoneman or without, we both agree that the armed forces, except for a very few at the top, are devoted to you. They can be counted on. All that we need to do is to make sure that they see the realities of the situation—that Mossy, the old bugger, smart-ass Riahi, the Tudeh and the Russians are trying to do you in. We get that across and we've nothing to worry about."

Metaphorically we patted ourselves on the back. I went on:

"Now, I've already mentioned our Iranian allies, or agents, if you wish to be more technical than they care to be—Boscoe One and Two. They are extremely competent, professional 'organizers' who have already demonstrated their competence."

The Shah nodded. I went no further, nor did I refer to our puzzlement over where and from whom the Boscoes had received their training. "Well, we count on them with confidence. They have a strong team under them"—no need to say we didn't know who made up that team—"they can distribute pamphlets, organize mobs, keep track of the oppostion—you name it, they'll do it. I know them personally and rely on them absolutely." It did not seem necessary to add that I never expected to see them again, that once the job was completed I hoped they would sink into their surroundings without a trace. They had no professional contact with foreigners—or, at least, so far as I could tell, with Americans, British or French. No way to guess who else they saw. But that was not my worry now.

"Incidentally, they seem to require almost no funds from us. We have a gigantic safe next to my principal assistant's office. It is in a big closet and occupies the whole space. This safe is jam-packed with stacks of rial notes. Your highest denomination note is only five hundred rials, and your current Prime Minister, for whose competence and reliability we have such regard," I said sarcastically, "has driven the exchange rate down so that it's worth just over five U.S. dollars. We have the equivalent of about one million dollars in that safe."*

Our allies and our money settled, I moved on to the fourth and final line of attack—what the Zahedis, father and son, had to contribute. The general was still hiding in the mountains east of Tajrish, just above a property the Zahedis then owned and on which Ardeshir later built a rather grand residence, with gardens and a fine swimming pool. At that time, however, there was just one small cabinlike building. One night Mustapha Vaysi and I climbed up the steep mountainside behind it for my first meeting with General Zahedi. There in a gully, which concealed his bedroll and a small lean-to, the general was encamped,

---

*During the operation we used less than $100,000 worth of rials.

with just one other man to keep him company. I suspected that there were more men scattered around behind the crags and in the ravines, but I saw no sign of them.

Our meeting was warm and friendly. However, there was difficulty in communication. The general spoke only Farsi and some German. I knew about as much German as he did and practically no Farsi. So much of our talk was through Mustapha, who interpreted at a breakneck pace. I explained all this to the Shah, who was suitably sympathetic.

"The Zahedis obviously have friends on whom they can rely. I'm sure they are all known to you." I strung off a list of names and H.I.M. nodded his approval. Once again the time had come to part, which we did with expressions—to put it formally—of mutual esteem.

For what remained of the week, I continued to meet with the Shah and, after each meeting, with Bill Herman and Nossey/Cafron in some place or other. They were now in regular touch with their friend, the emissary who had set up my first meeting with H.I.M. I explained to them that I would need to get some documents into the Shah's hands no later than early morning of August 9, when we had agreed he would be taking off for the Caspian. They assured me there would be no problem. Our sessions with them had continued to be interesting and, most particularly, divertingly amusing. Our Iranian friends could always come up with some zany bit of hilarity. Tension, I noted, seemed to require and often to generate excuse for laughter.

Finally affairs came to their head. On midnight of August 8–9, the Shah and I had what was scheduled to be our final discussion. We had agreed on all the necessary objectives, procedures, tactics—the works. The *firmans*, I promised, would be delivered so that he could sign them the next morning. After that he was scheduled to fly to the Caspian, along with Queen Soraya, to await results.

It seemed to me appropriate that I should deliver a parting message from President Eisenhower. Since he had neglected to send one, I put into words what he must surely be feeling.

"Your Majesty, I received earlier this evening a cable from Washington. President Eisenhower had asked that I convey to you this word: 'I wish Your Imperial Majesty godspeed. If the Pahlavis and the Roosevelts working together cannot solve this little problem, then there is no hope anywhere. I have complete faith that you will get this done!'"

We agreed that the President had summed things up very well. Thus cheered and mutually fortified, we parted in good spirits.

I went back to join Bill, Nossey and Cafron, for once assembled at Bill's house to celebrate. The moon was high, full and bright. Trees and mountains rose above me, soft in the dark. The world seemed benign, promising good things to come. How was I to know that within twelve hours I would feel disturbed, within thirty-six profoundly uneasy and in one week downright desperate?

CHAPTER
11

"Give not a windy night a rainy morrow."
William Shakespeare (d. 1616)

It must have been about five o'clock in the morning of August 9 when I finally tumbled into bed. Four hours later I was awakened by the sound of Bill cursing in the next room. Quite out of character—he was normally a mild-mannered chap—he was using distinctly blue language. I extricated myself from the sheets in which I had become tangled and struggled to the door.

"What in God's name is the matter?" I inquired crossly.

He gave me a black look. "The fat-ass to whom N. and C. gave the *firmans*"—I am cleaning up his words for family readership—"he loused things up to a fare-thee-well. Would you believe it? He didn't get them to the palace until after the Shah took off for the Caspian!"

I sat down with a thud. "What in [expurgated] do we do now, for Christ's sake?"

Bill sat down too. After a moment's thought he became more practical. "We'll have to get hold of Colonel Nassiry." (Nematollah Nassiry was commander of the Imperial Bodyguard at the Shah's palace.) "He can get another airplane and fly the damn documents to Ramsar, or Kelardesht, or wherever the Shah is finally at. But how the hell do we get hold of Nassiry?"

That of course had to be done through Nossey and Cafron. We managed to reach them and bully them into action. The *firmans* were still at the palace, and "fat ass" did communicate their whereabouts to Nassiry. He in turn flew them north. Thus, a bit behind schedule, the *firmans* and the Shah were finally together at the Caspian. But the weather closed in. Clouds and fog swathed the mountains north of Teheran. There was no way Nassiry could fly back with the precious documents.

Mossadegh had imposed a curfew from 9:00 P.M. until six in the morning, but in any case there was little to draw us from the Herman compound. So we sat, in the daytime around the pool, after dark in the living room, smoking, drinking mild vodkas with lime juice, playing hearts with the children or backgammon with each other, and cursing heartfelt obscenities at unpredictable intervals.

Finally, long after curfew on the night of Wednesday, August 12, there was a violent pounding on the compound gates. It was close to midnight, but Bill and I were still up, nervously talking about anything irrelevant that calmed our worries, puffing cigarettes and sipping our drinks. The pounding startled us, filled us with what we thought irrational hope. We hurried out to investigate. When we opened the gates in streamed a horde of grimy, unshaven Iranians, most of whom we'd never seen before—Nassiry was not among them—but if they had never seen us before, it didn't matter. They knew who we were, and each of them hugged and kissed us with the greatest enthusiasm. What seemed like an eternity passed before we could discover what it was all about. They had just driven across the mountains from the Caspian, and they had the signed *firmans* with them. It was *our* turn to embrace *them*.

But when we started to communicate coherently—not an easy task—we got a rude shock. Nothing could be done, they assured us with finality, until Saturday evening, three nights later. Thursday afternoon and all of Friday make up the Iranian weekend, and they were certain that the *firmans* could not be delivered and that no effective action would be possible before Saturday. Bill and I were already nervous about the delay and the increased chances of betrayal that every extra hour might mean. But there seemed no choice; unhappily, reluctantly, we accepted the enforced wait. Long nerve-racking hours, with no action possible, lay ahead of us.

August 13 and 14—Thursday and Friday—we continued our dreary routine, more nervous than ever. The pool was no solace, cigarettes and vodka-limes tasted awful. We could think of nothing to talk about that was neither dreary and boring nor insanely alarming. Worst of all, there was nothing useful to do. Whether or not it had been necessary, our Iranian colleagues had effectively made the two days a period of total inactivity. We could only endure them; we could not escape.

Saturday seemed to take forever in arriving, and once it did arrive, morning and afternoon went more slowly than anything we had ever before lived through.

As the time grew near when we were to proceed downtown, we went to the house of colleagues nearby in Tajrish for a final conference. There being nothing meaningful to confer about, we had another vodka and lime and played the record of "Luck Be a Lady Tonight" from *Guys and Dolls*, which immediately became our theme song for the occasion. Then we went "rolling down the mountain," as another old song has it, full of hope and hilarity.

On the way into the city, we drove right by General Riahi's house, without seeing any indication that things had gone wrong. When we reached Bill's headquarters, it was still light, although curfew was about to begin. There were no visible troop movements, ominous or otherwise. We settled down in his office, prepared for a long vigil, which—hopefully—would be ended by a phone call from Colonel Nassiry reporting successful delivery of the *firmans* to Mossadegh *and* to Zahedi.

As time passed by, hilarity diminished and we grew increasingly nervous. Early on we were alarmed because there were no signs of activity. Later we became alarmed by such signs. We could hear the clank and clatter of moving tanks. These continued for some time, then stopped completely. A telephone call should now have come, assuring us that everything had proceeded according to plan. But no call came. It was by then well past midnight. In spite of the late hour Bill began to telephone various friends whose houses or apartments looked out on the main thoroughfare, Takht-i-Jamshid. Most of them had nothing to report, but one, whose house was fairly close to that of Mossadegh, told Bill that he could see tanks and other vehicles, filled with soldiers, lined up outside Mossadegh's house. Of course he could not distinguish whose tanks they were. At first we were optimistic, but an hour passed and we heard nothing from those who were supposed to communicate with us; we grew increasingly depressed.

Dawn came, and we turned on our radio. At six there was no sound from it. Then at seven o'clock the radio came to life. There was a blare of military music and an announcement in Farsi in which we thought we could distinguish the word "Mossadegh."

Hastily summoning our nearby interpreter, we listened to the broadcast. Mossadegh came on the air himself and announced that there had been an attempt by the Shah, encouraged by "foreign elements," to displace the Prime Minister. Mossadegh was therefore "obliged" to take all power to himself.

What had happened, though it took us some days to fill in all the details, was just what we had feared: *Betrayal.* Some young officer—we never did identify him—went to General Riahi's house on Saturday afternoon. I do not believe that he was part of our group; Peter Stoneman insisted vehemently that he could not have been. But at the very least one of Peter's recruits had talked unwisely and to the wrong man. In any case, the informant was able to tell Riahi enough to alert him immediately. The general sped down to the city to assemble all the forces he could get together. It is important—perhaps I should say it *was* most important then—to recognize that the troops Riahi did assemble knew nothing of what was really happening. They were simply told that an upstart colonel was going to seek to overthrow the Prime Minister. He should be arrested and brought to the general's office at once. If we had known what actually happened it might have given us hope. Since we knew nothing, we were close to despair.

The true sequence of events was this: Our Colonel Nassiry set off with his small force of tanks from Saadabad Palace at about ten-thirty in the evening. What with one delay and another, it was eleven when he reached Riahi's house, more than halfway into the city on Kharia (avenue) Pahlavi. No one, not even a servant, not even an orderly, was there. Mystified, concerned but undaunted, Nassiry proceeded along his planned course. That he had been unable to arrest Riahi before delivering the *firmans* dismissing Mossadegh did not in any way deter him. But when he arrived in front of the Prime Minister's home on Takht-e-Jamshid, just a few blocks west of our embassy, he found all the troops that General Riahi could gather lined up to receive him. If they had obeyed Riahi's orders literally, as he had meant them to be obeyed, Nassiry would have got no farther. But when he announced that he had a royal *firman* to deliver, under the Shah's orders, to Premier Mossadegh, there was some indecision among those confronting him. Finally they decided to let him deposit his *firman* before arresting him. This compromise was all he needed.

Marching boldly up to Mossadegh's residence, he pounded on the door. A servant answered, not as sleepy-looking as might have been expected at midnight. Nassiry demanded to see the Prime Minister. The servant answered that he was asleep, could not be disturbed.

"Then take this decree from His Imperial Majesty to Dr. Mossadegh immediately," Nassiry insisted. The servant, appearing to be somewhat flustered by the demand, took the *firman* and vanished, shutting the door firmly with Nassiry still on the outside. Finally the servant returned and opened the door.

"The Prime Minister says to go away," he said in a faintly quavering voice.

"I want a receipt," Nassiry replied.

"I'm to give you one myself, if you have something for me to write it on."

Nassiry took a piece of paper from his pocket. On it

he wrote: "Received from Col. Nassiry of His Imperial Majesty's royal bodyguard: one *firman*, ordering the dismissal from office of Dr. Mohammed Mossadegh, until now Prime Minister to H.I.M. Signed on behalf of Dr. Mossadegh, ———"

The servant signed, and Nassiry turned back to the officer commanding the troops General Riahi had sent. "Take me to General Riahi," he said formally. Without more ado, they did.

Once at the general's headquarters, Nassiry behaved with courage and dignity. Riahi accused the commander of the imperial guards of "dangerous action," of attempting to foment rebellion, of planning a *coup d'état*.

"Nonsense!" replied Nassiry. "You are the one who is guilty of dangerous action. I am simply carrying out the Shah's orders, insofar as you have given me opportunity to do so. I have still a *firman* to deliver to General Zahedi, appointing him Prime Minister to take Dr. Mossadegh's place. You have no right to interfere with my carrying out the instructions I have been given by H.I.M." He showed Riahi the receipt from Mossadegh's servant and the *firman* naming Zahedi to be P.M. Angry, Riahi observed that it was unusual to deliver orders in the middle of the night. Nassiry countered by asking if it were any better etiquette for him to be interrogated at such an early hour in the morning. Riahi ignored the question, placed Nassiry under arrest, had him stripped of his uniform and imprisoned. For the moment, at least, Riahi must have been sure he had the situation under control. Indeed he did have things under control, but only until we turned on our radio in the chancery at 6:00 A.M. and heard Dr. Mossadegh's broadcast at 7:00.

Once we had grasped what ancient Dr. Mossadegh was telling his fellow Iranians, we began numbering the most important things we must do *at once*. Before we could actually start doing any of them, the phone rang. It was Dick Manville, and he had a lot to report.

"Guess who has shown up at my house? It is Mustapha Vaysi. He went to look for you, Kim, at Bill's home, and when he couldn't find you there he came to mine. He is now here."

"Hang onto him, Dick! Bill," I promised, "will pick up the only two American journalists whom we know to be in Teheran. He will take them to your house for a brief interview with Mustapha, who will tell them that the Shah has dismissed Mossadegh and appointed Zahedi in his place. Then he will bring Mustapha into the embassy compound." I suggested to Bill that he follow the example set by my first visit to meet with H.I.M. at the palace, when I had entered the grounds concealed under a rug in the back of the car.

"Mustapha has also told me where General Zahedi is. He has been spending the night at an apartment—" Dick gave the address—"which is not very far from the embassy. I suggest that one of you pick him up as quickly as possible. If Bill is coming here, perhaps you can do it, Kim."

"O.K. I'll collect him as soon as I can arrange a 'safe house' to stash him away in. I'll try Fred Zimmerman." Fred was one of our group who had been out of action with hepatitis the whole time I had been in Teheran. His house was not far from our office and the embassy. It had a big basement. It was also surrounded by a high wall. It seemed like an ideal place to keep the good general under safe cover.

I had thought that Dick was through, but he had one further item to report.

"Just before I called you, I had a call from an Iranian friend of mine whom you have not met, Kim, although I believe I have mentioned him to you. His name is Mohsen Tahuyi. Apparently I've been a bit indiscreet with him. Anyhow, he has guessed that we have something in the works and he is now volunteering his help."

"You're sure he's completely reliable? Then I think we should certainly take him up on it." Actually, Mohsen Tahuyi, whose help we accepted so casually, turned out to provide invaluable aid throughout the remainder of the operation. We arranged that Dick, as soon as Mustapha's interview was over, would pick him up and bring him, also under a blanket, into the compound.

"You know we've already made arrangements to have that small radio shack, which should be quite secure, and which has living quarters for the operator as well as a room for the radio." The radio *and* the American operator had been moved for better security into the basement of another building. The operator, now our only link with the outside world, was necessarily aware of what was going on. He could not have been more cooperative. We had already made arrangements with him for the use of his shack for whatever purposes we might need it. Now it appeared that we would need it very badly.

So Bill took off in a rush for Dick's house, which was up close to his own in nearby Tajrish, borrowing a car from a member of the embassy staff so that I could pick up the general in his own car. I got in touch with Fred, who, though still hepatitic, was most agreeable. He promised the use of his basement and said that he himself would bring down meals to his visitor and see to his wants as best he could. Since Fred's house was only three blocks to the east of our headquarters, it could not have been more convenient. I expressed suitable gratitude for his offer.

Now I took off to collect the good general. It was a bit awkward knocking on the door of a stranger's apartment, looking for the most wanted character in

Iran, but I could not afford to let it bother me. Actually, Zahedi opened the door himself. He had a suitcase already packed—I later discovered it contained his uniform—and he was dressed in nondescript trousers and sweater. Once I got him safely into the car, I covered him with another one of those invaluable blankets and drove, at a sedate pace, to Fred's compound. The gates safely closed behind us, Fred and I escorted the general to his cellar quarters. Fortunately Fred spoke a bit more German than I did, so that communications between the two were possible if not fluent. I left them happily together.

Returning to headquarters, I checked the radio shack and found that not only were Bill and Mustapha there, but Dick had also arrived with Mohsen Tahuyi. I sent Bill back to his office, where he arrived just in time to receive a frantic call from Nossey and Cafron. They felt themselves to be in considerable danger and wanted to be picked up on a designated street corner *immediately.* By that time, we were used to providing a most effective taxi service, and we also had the blanket routine down cold. So the two were brought into our battle station in the usual fashion.

We soon established a pretty demanding work schedule. What we obviously needed was a good number of copies of the two *firmans,* particularly the one appointing Zahedi as Prime Minister. Dick produced a Persian typewriter and some stencil sheets, and we set Mohsen Tahuyi to work typing copies of the *firmans.* We had a few photostats of the originals, but photostating equipment was not readily available to be used in the shack, so we had to make do with stencils. They did prove to be suitably effective.

Nonetheless, the process took time. Bill and Dick went out to collect refreshments, food and drink, for our crew. It was well after dark when we had finished the task of reproducing the *firmans.* People stretched themselves out on the floor to be as comfortable as possible and to try to get some sleep. I was restless, however, and spent what seemed like an unnecessarily long number of hours picking up all the debris and sorting the papers into manageable piles. The bulk of the *firmans* were to go to the Boscoe brothers for distribution, and a certain number were reserved for other allies. We also kept two copies of each *firman* for Mustapha and Mohsen, to whom we had assigned a special mission. Mustapha was to go to Isfahan to seek the support of the military commander there. Mohsen would drive to Kermanshah to enlist support of the local commander, who had tanks and armored vehicles under his command. Mohsen knew the colonel quite well; he described him as an ambitious man who would seize any chance to make himself nationally prominent. Thus we felt most hopeful that his response would be favorable.

So we collected two cars without diplomatic plates for them—one the personal car of Bill's driver, a small Fiat, the other a large Packard belonging, most inappropriately, to Dick's tiny wife. Since Mohsen was slight in frame and Mustapha practically a giant, Mohsen got the Fiat, Mustapha the Packard. As soon as the curfew was lifted on Monday morning, they took off.

Just as they were leaving, the Tudeh, with strong Russian encouragement, took to the streets. "Took over" the streets would be no exaggeration, even though there were no more than several thousand of them. They ranged over the whole city north and west of the bazaar, screaming antiroyalist slogans, hacking away at statues of the old Shah Reza Khan and his son Mohammed Reza Shah, and, incidentally but most joyfully, looting everything they could grab, every shop or building they could break into. At the time, frankly, it scared the hell out of me. And it must have cheered the Russians. But soon I recognized that this was the best thing we could have hoped for. The more they shouted against the Shah, the more the army and the people recognized them as the enemy. If *they* hated the Shah, then army and people hated them. And the more they ravaged the city, the more they angered the great bulk of its inhabitants. Nothing could have dramatized the guts of the conflict more effectively or more rapidly. On Sunday there had been some rioting and pillaging, but Monday put the frosting on the cake. Give them time to get ready and the Teheranis would surely rise to smite them. And the Boscoe brothers would provide inspiration.

But for the time being, Bill and I were once again left with nothing to do but wait. We had no fingernails left to bite, no kids to play hearts with, and lime juice was in short supply. There was vodka aplenty but good reason for caution in its consumption. What we did have that we had not enjoyed before was the uninter-rupted companionship of Nossey and Cafron. This made waiting, I suppose, less boring but certainly not more pleasant. "Laughing Boy" prattled on forever in Farsi, and the "Mad Musician," lacking any instru-ment such as his player piano on which to express himself without words, kept up a continuous chatter. Often he chattered in English, which we understood too easily. The whole routine did get on our nerves a bit.

We sought any possible way to keep ourselves busy. There were some useful things we *could* do. For one, we could communicate with the Boscoes. Our emissar-ies, successful or not, would have to return by Tuesday evening, so we advised the brothers that Wednesday, August 19, 28 Mordad, must be The Day. In reply they sent word that they were ready, that they would act. Their principal targets would be Mossadegh's house, where Nassiry had already tried and failed, and the

Teheran radio station, about halfway up the Old Shemiran Road in the direction of Tajrish, where Bill and Dick both lived. Their communication had to be brief, so they could give no details of what they planned; we simply had to be ready to support them as best we could. The best thing we could hope for was to provide the troops moving in from "off stage," either from Isfahan or Kermanshah—if possible from both. We sent an additional message telling them that. Then, having done all we could do, we simply gnawed our fingertips where the nails had been. It wasn't much, but it was better than nothing.

"God save us," said Bill with uncustomary piety. "Do you realize that if we're lucky, and that's a big if, we'll have only thirty-six hours of Nossey–Cafron listening to endure?" Put that way, it didn't sound too bad. Just awful.

Eventually, of course, it had to end.

First we faced disappointment. Mustapha Vaysi, weary and pale under a coating of thin desert dust, arrived to report a total bust. He is a very persuasive chap, but on the commanding officer in Isfahan he had been unable to make a dent. The man was just too cautious. He accepted the *firman* as genuine; he merely questioned its effectiveness. Carefully, precisely, he had explained that he was not anti-Shah, nor was he pro-Mossadegh. He was simply unwilling at this point to commit himself to either.

"He's plain scared to death," said Mustapha pungently. "If he makes a choice, he's sure he'll choose the loser, and that he does *not* want to do." We were all in the depths of gloom when Mohsen Tahuyi arrived. We didn't need to wait for a word, for his face told it all: success!

"The colonel will move. Tomorrow at dawn. He'll come with tanks and armored cars, ready to fight if necessary. In fact he may have to fight to get here, because I think the Tudeh are very strong in Hamadan." (Hamadan, two hundred miles away, is halfway between Teheran and Kermanshah.) "But he'll take care of them." Mohsen was alight with triumph, and we glowed with him. What matter when the colonel should arrive, we had what we needed, and we could spread it throughout Teheran—the news of troops moving off stage should give the Boscoe brothers all the support they would need. Once their own actions had begun, all the city—army and people—would take to the streets in support.

This was, to be sure, the showdown. And that night was the final bit of waiting that Bill and I would have to endure. If it proved to be in vain, then all was lost. But then, we would have been wrong about everything, and so far it looked as though we'd been right. We allowed no room for thoughts of failure. In fact, we had absolutely no plans for what we should do if the morrow produced a dud.

Meanwhile, poor Loy Henderson, "exiled" to Switzerland, had been entirely cut off from news of developments. All he had was news reporting, largely irrelevant; there were *no* official cables for him, State or CIA. The day on which we had originally proposed action went by—and *nothing* happened. Loy grew ever more restless, nervous. Finally, on August 14, he could stand Switzerland no longer. He flew to Beirut, no more relaxing but at least closer to the scene. It was there, on the morning of August 16, that he heard of Mossadegh's radio speech to the nation. Later that morning the Shah's departure from Iran was reported. Henderson wasted no time. Commandeering an embassy plane from Beirut, he took off at once for Teheran. On his arrival he went, of course, straight to the embassy. But his Counselor of Embassy knew no more—or not as much—of what was happening than he did. He sent for Bill Herman, who was after all on his staff. When Bill was finally found, he suggested that the Ambassador had best talk to me.

Late Monday evening I made my way cautiously through the compound to the residence where, on a terrace by the swimming pool, Loy awaited me, alone, impatiently.

"We've run into some small complications," I explained rather unnecessarily. "However, I think we have things under control. Two or three days should see things developing our way."

"Meanwhile," said the Ambassador with understandable concern, "what in heaven's name do I do?"

I refrained from saying that he might have observed our agreement and stayed away. "Probably you will have to see Dr. Mossadegh. Now that you're here, I don't see how that can be avoided."

Loy grunted. "And what in heaven's name do I say?"

"My suggestion would be that you complain about the way Americans here are being harassed. Anonymous telephone calls saying 'Yankee go home!' or calling them obscene names. Even if a child picks up the phone the caller just shouts dirty words at him." Respect for Ambassadorial sensitivities prevented me from giving particular examples.

Loy responded vigorously. "That's fine. I'll certainly do it. But what if he asks me about American support for the Shah?"

"I think you should tell him that while Americans do not want to, and will not, get involved in the domestic politics of a foreign country, they are bound to be sympathetic to the man they regard as the legitimate sovereign."

The Ambassador considered my suggestion with care. "I don't want to appear to be taking sides too much. But certainly the Shah is chief of state; it is only proper, and natural, that we should sympathize with him. However, I will make it quite plain that we have no intention of interfering in the internal affairs of a friendly country."

To this noble sentiment I made no comment. Diplomats are expected, if not required, to say such things.

So on Tuesday afternoon, while Mustapha and Mohsen were just about completing their missions to rouse help for their monarch, Ambassador Henderson called on the man who still claimed the title of Prime Minister. He was received with acrimony and a slew of complaints.

The old man shrilled at him: "What *are* your citizens saying about my country? Why are they criticizing it, trying to work against it, voicing their support for a tyrant who has wisely, if somewhat cravenly, fled to foreign lands? This is most improper. They have no business trying to pressure us in any way, particularly on behalf of a man who is now no more than a rebel!"

Loy could not resist a very pointed reply. Although he did, in my nondiplomatic view, address his ancient, lachrymose adversary overpolitely and incorrectly as "Mr. Prime Minister," he hit a vulnerable point with full force.

"You talk of His Majesty's flight," he said coolly. He made the same point the Shah had made to me. "As a Christian, may I remind a Moslem of the tradition started by Prophet Mohammed, after whom you are named, in his famous 'flight'—the Hegira, in 622 by our calendar, I believe—from Mecca. Your calendar begins from that date, the starting point of Islam. The point I wish to make is that the Prophet fled not from fear but to dramatize a point. The Hegira marked the rise of Islam as a world force. His Majesty's Hegira may mark *his* rise also!"

Mossadegh looked discomfited, but Loy gave him no time to respond. And Loy grew no more "diplomatic" as he proceeded: "My fellow citizens are understandably disturbed at seeing a man whom they have regarded as the friendly chief of a friendly state sent into exile—for reasons which," he added sharply, "they don't understand any more than do I."

Observing with satisfaction the effect of his remarks, Loy went on: "Furthermore I must tell you that my fellow citizens are being harassed most unpleasantly. Not only do they get threatening telephone calls, often answered by their children who are then subjected to rude words children should not even hear. Not only are they insulted on the streets when going peacefully about their business; in addition to all the verbal aggression they are exposed to, their automobiles are damaged whenever they are left exposed. Parts are stolen, headlights are smashed, tires are deflated"—Mossadegh looked puzzled by that word, but Henderson did not pause to explain it—"and if the cars are left unlocked their upholstery is cut to pieces.

"Unless this kind of harassment is stopped, Your Excellency, I am going to ask my government to recall all dependents and also all men whose presence here is not required in our own national interest."

Visibly shaken by the force of Loy's expression, the old gentleman became confused, almost apologetic.

"I would not want you to do that, Mr. Ambassador. Let me call my police chief. I'll see that your compatriots are given proper protection." Before Loy had taken his leave, the police had been called and given their instructions. Later, Loy and I were to agree that this indeed had been a helpful move, encouraging the pro-Shah police force. For the time being, however, I was still restricted—except for a cautious ambassadorial evening visit—to the radio shack. And by the next time I saw Loy there was much else to talk about.

CHAPTER 12

"An optimist is a man who says the bottle
is half full when it's half empty."

Anonymous

In point of fact,
Wednesday did not start off with a bang or a whimper
either. The Boscoe brothers did get their "thing"
moving early, but it began in the bazaar, a long way
away from where Bill and I waited so impatiently.
There the Boscoes had enlisted the support of the
Zirkaneh giants—the famous weightlifters who make a
ritual of their act. Now, assembled at the north
entrance to the bazaar, these huge figures started
marching westward, shouting and twirling more like
dervishes than what they actually were. The younger
Boscoe, who was the contact with them, saw no reason
why, since they could hardly take their enormous

barbells with them, they should feel in any way restricted. Apparently they did not.

The one thing that did give us tremendous encouragement in those early hours was the Tabriz radio. (Azerbaijan borders on the Soviet Union; its support was significant.) We did not hear, nor could we have understood, the broadcast itself. But from eight o'clock on a number of friends called in, asking, elatedly, "Did you hear Tabriz?"

"No," I replied to the first. "I'm afraid not. What did it say?"

"Tabriz is one hundred percent behind the Shah! Zindabad Shah!"

"Long live the Shah!" I repeated with enthusiasm. Bill and I did a small celebrating dance in the hall outside his office, the office being too tiny to contain our excitement. Word that Bakhtiar was on the march, we soon heard, was also circulating throughout the city. Even though Teheran radio was playing things very cozy and by ten o'clock was reduced to a dull quotation of grain prices, things were clearly moving well, in the right direction. There was little traffic on Takht-e-Jamshid, but soon Dick came in from Tajrish. Looking out the window onto the avenue, he commented on the lack of cars.

"Coming down the mountain, drivers are blowing their horns and cheering. If you don't have a picture of the Shah in your windshield, people shout at you to stick a ten-rial note under the wiper." He took a bill from his pocket and waved it at us. It did show a handsome portrait of H.I.M. "If you don't have a wiper—and if you've been parking in the streets lately you probably don't—you wedge it in the corner or stick it in front of your rear-view mirror. You should still have one of those!" He was literally bubbling over with joy, and we did another dance in the hallway.

"Why don't you go out and have a look around?" I suggested to Bill.

He took his secretary with him, I suppose on the theory that a couple would somehow look less suspicious than a lone man. They returned every bit as enthusiastic as Dick had been.

"You can look down Takht-e-Jamshid toward the bazaar and see signs of a huge mob approaching. They are cheering and they are waving banners. The Zirkaneh are in sight and everyone is shouting 'Zindabad Shah.'"

"Do you think the time has come to turn General Zahedi loose to lead the crowd?" Dick asked the question that was on all our minds. We gave it some thought.

Reluctantly, I said I thought we should hold off just a bit longer. "There is nothing to be gained by rushing. Let's wait till the crowd gets to Mossadegh's house. That should be a good moment for our hero to make his appearance."

Mustapha and Mohsen had already left the radio shack, and, when we checked, Nossey and Cafron were also on the point of departure. "Laughing Boy" was in high spirits and the "Mad Musician" said they were going off to rouse their friends into action.

"I am not sure where Mustapha is headed. He doesn't know where General Zahedi is, does he?"

I assured the two that he did not and they nodded, disappointed but understanding.

"Mohsen says he's going to collect a 'task force'"— the musical one was proud of the military expressions he had picked up, and practically smirked as he pronounced this one—"which force he plans to lead up the mountain to take over the radio station."

I nodded. This was quite according to plan. Mohsen had told us that on The Day his target was to broadcast, at the earliest possible moment, that Zahedi had taken power and the Shah was on his way back. That his words might be a bit ahead of the actual events did not bother him in the least.

Another period of waiting was in order, but this at least could be filled with activity—distracting if not really productive. Dick was constantly slipping off to check progress along Takht-e-Jamshid and reporting back that, though to his impatient eyes it was slow, real progress could be discerned. Bill kept the telephone busy with calls to friends—somewhat like his calls of the previous Saturday night but this time *much* more encouraging. From all over the city there were reports of movement, this time favorable movement. Once when he left the telephone briefly idle, "Mad Musician" got through, in a state of joyous excitement.

"Things are really crackling, Bill!" At least Bill thought the word was "crackling," though it could have been "cracking." We had no idea what the Persian version would have been. "Is there anything in particular you'd like us to do?"

"Sure. Cross your fingers. Dance a jig."

"What do you mean?"

"Knock on wood. Do whatever you can think of to keep things crackling *our* way." Bill was so elated he didn't care what he was saying. "Mad Musician" recognized this and gave a high-pitched cackle of approval. Then he hung up and took off to do God knows what. Our contact with N. and C. throughout the day was enthusiastic but, to us, totally incomprehensible.

But there was one event that we could all understand. As the Teheran radio droned dully on quoting the same old grain prices, our radio operator came up from the bowels of the building we had moved him to. It was quarter past eleven. Tears streaming down his cheeks, he handed me a message. It was from the Under Secretary of State, the Honorable Walter Bedell Smith, my raspy-voiced, sharp-tongued friendly enemy, or critical ally, "Beedle." He had, I discovered later, already tried to send the same message twenty-four hours earlier, but it had been returned to him by my stalwart British colleague on Cyprus, which was our relay point. This time Beedle had really blasted Henry Montague, who, most reluctantly, had felt obliged to follow Beedle's instructions. All our communications were at this time coming through Cyprus, which for some days had had no word from us. Henry had faith, or, if one wishes to be cynical, nothing to lose. The British were totally out of Iran. The AIOC had lost; no more could be taken from them. But Beedle did not want the Americans' hand exposed, particularly in failure. He assumed that no word from me was bad word, and he felt I should get *out*. Under the circumstances I could hardly blame him. Had the message arrived earlier—when, in fact, he first sent it—I should have had a real problem. Now I was just about home free.

"Never mind, chum," I said to the radio man. "Buried underground as you are, you have no way of knowing. But—" I coined no new phrase—"*the tide has turned*. Things are going our way. Right will triumph. All for the best, in the best of possible worlds." Running out of optimistic aphorisms, I clapped him on the shoulder and sent him back downstairs, confused but greatly encouraged. Immediately I sat down and composed my reply, knowing it could not possibly be sent for some hours but hoping it could be sent then.

Beedle's message said in effect, "Give up and get out." Mine responded: "Yours of 18 August received. Happy to report R. N. Ziegler [the pseudonym for Zahedi] safely installed and KGSAVOY [the cryptonym for the Shah] will be returning to Teheran in triumph shortly. Love and kisses from all the team." Satisfied, grinning from ear to ear, I sat back to do some more waiting—with as much patience as I could muster.

By now the crowd of demonstrators, including many uniformed soldiers and police, was streaming past our chancery. Its vanguard had already reached Mossadegh's house, some half a dozen blocks beyond us. The crackle of rifles, and the *boom-thud* of an occasional mortar, could clearly be heard. There was nothing I could contribute, and I was getting ravenously hungry. So I walked into the embassy compound past the Ambassador's residence to the Counselor of Embassy's house. He and his wife were old friends of mine. Discreetly, they asked no questions about what was going on, but gave me the drink and the lunch I so obviously needed. Their radio, I noticed, was still stuck on those damned grain prices. Surely Mohsen would be changing that soon.

In fact someone else beat him to the radio station, someone—I never discovered who it was—who had exactly the same idea and friends to help him carry it out. The first signs were odd. The tempo of the price quotations slowed, as if the announcer were falling asleep. Gradually, agonizingly, the sound grated to a halt. For what seemed an eternity, there was dead silence. My hosts and I stared at one another in puzzlement. Then a voice—not that of Mohsen—came on the air. Once again we heard the shout "Zindabad Shah! Long live the Shah!" And, alternating Farsi and English, our unknown speaker came out with the well-intended lies, or "pre-truths," which Mohsen had been planning to broadcast.

"The Shah's instruction that Mossadegh be dismissed has been carried out. The new Prime Minister, Fazlollah Zahedi, is now in office. And His Imperial Majesty is on his way home!"

Getting to my feet, I *believe* I thanked the Counselor

and his wife most politely for an excellent lunch. What I *know* is that I was on my way to pick up General Zahedi, to deliver him to whatever point from which he thought he could best assume command. As I hurried along a sudden thought struck me and made me hurry even more. Why had the man who took over the radio station "translated" the essential words of his declaration into English? That was not a normal thing to do. I doubted even if Mohsen Tahuyi would have done it. But a Boscoe brother could well have told the broadcaster to include those few words just to make sure that I got the point—and got moving. I moved.

There was one interruption, a most useful one, before I reached General Zahedi in his basement. As I hurried through our gate and turned left on Takht-e-Jamshid to head for Fred Zimmerman's house, I was engulfed in the crowd moving west (to my right) on the avenue. They were headed, full of the best intentions, for Dr. Mossadegh's house several blocks away. And in their midst I spotted a figure in full uniform—the general in command of the air force. I remembered the last meeting in John Foster Dulles' office.

"What about General Guilanshah?" he had asked. I could see again his faint grin at my surprise; I could also remember my reply that I could see no role for the general. Now I damn well could.

He had recognized me at the same time I'd caught sight of him. We fought our way through the mob until we could communicate. He gave me a broad smile.

"There must be something I can do to help."

I sought for no explanation of his question but responded quickly, "Damn right there is! Pick up a tank if you can and meet me one block west of here in fifteen minutes. I'll be in a small black Citroën, and I'll turn over General Zahedi to your care."

His eyes gleamed. "Where is he now?"

Without thinking, I told him. If I'd thought, I probably would have been more discreet. But who can say whether it was a mistake or not. Anyhow we parted quickly, hurrying in opposite directions.

Arriving at Fred's compound, I went directly to the cellar. There I found the legal—about to become actual—Prime Minister of Iran sitting in what looked to me like his winter underwear. His uniform was draped over a chair beside him. Once again we communicated in our poor German, but I had no difficulty in getting my message across. He rose immediately and started pulling on the uniform over his heavy woolens. Just as he was buttoning up his tunic we heard loud rumbling and clanking in the courtyard above us. Men were cheering, and there was much Persian chatter. The door to the cellar burst open. I could recognize Guilanshah's voice.

There was barely time for me to conceal myself behind the basement furnace before a stream of shouting Iranians came tumbling down the steps. At the sight of Zahedi they roared and rushed forward, embracing him, lifting him on their shoulders and pounding up the staircase to the yard. Apparently there were two or three tanks—I couldn't tell how many—revving their motors in the yard. The crowd draped themselves all over them, holding Zahedi high on one, and went clattering through the gateway straight on to Takht-e-Jamshid. As they appeared on the avenue I heard a great shout from the crowd, which followed them tumultuously as they headed off in the direction of Mossadegh's residence.

As I learned later but did not know then, they didn't reach old Mossy's house until he had already fled—over the garden wall and into a house from which he somehow managed to vanish. It was not until several days later that he called in to the police station—hoping for help, perhaps—and gave himself up.

At this point there was nothing I could think of to do

to be helpful. So I forced my way through the crowd, which was notably, cheerfully, friendly, back to our headquarters. We were no longer occupying the radio shack but had moved again into Bill's small office. There he, Dick and I poured ourselves small celebratory drinks (the supply of vodka in Bill's office seemed inexhaustible) to toast impending victory. Actually, to all intents and purposes, it was no longer impending but won. Our colonel from the west would not reach Teheran until evening, but the rumor of his movement had given us all we needed. The actual arrival of his troops simply added more enthusiasm to a town already drunk with victory.

Mohsen Tahuyi called in to say that someone else had beat him to the radio station but that he could not have done a better job himself. Where, he asked, did I think he could find Mustapha?

"Damned if I know. We put General Zahedi on the streets, on top of a tank"—I looked at my watch—"just about an hour ago. He was going to Mossadegh's house."

"The old gent's escaped somehow. God knows where he is. I hear that the general—the new Prime Minister, excuse me," he said, laughing—"has gone to the Officers' Club. Probably Mustapha, *and* Ardeshir, are with him by now. I'll look for them there."

"Good luck. And if you do find them, please be kind enough to let us know."

Mohsen laughed again. "I'll promise to be kind. I think you've earned more than a little kindness, Kim! *Salam aleykum.* God be with you."

"*Aleykum a salam.*" He hung up; I was confident he would be calling back soon.

Sure enough, Fazlollah Zahedi, now effectively as well as legally Prime Minister, had indeed gone to the Officers' Club. Ardeshir and Mustapha also apparently had no difficulty in finding him, and by the time

Mohsen got there the process of forming a cabinet was well under way. Because of Ardeshir's relationship to the general, he was not to be included, although it was clearly hoped that H.I.M., soon after his return, would find some suitable appointment for him. Mustapha and Mohsen were both appointed to cabinet positions; the other ministers were known to me only by name, but they were a distinguished group. I was soon to meet them all, formally, in a most informal manner.

Once again there was a waiting period, this time filled with jubilation, celebration, and occasional totally unpredictable whacks on the back as one or the other of us was suddenly overcome with enthusiasm. Bill and I wandered over to the Chancery. Those in the embassy were now well aware that something "good" had happened, though they had no idea that we were in any small way responsible. And the room to which we had just been guided, in the western end of the top floor of the Chancery, was isolated enough to give us some privacy. The Ambassador was keeping to himself in the residence, but the counselor and other senior staff members had come to the Chancery. Whoever might have been responsible for the happy events, they clearly called for celebration. Bill, Dick and I saw no reason not to join them, though one of us was always keeping an eye on the gate to spot the arrival of any of our Iranian friends.

Finally it was Ardeshir himself who drove into the courtyard. He tooted his horn exuberantly, and I hurried down to him.

"I am here in place of Mustapha, who is almost as busy as I am!"

We embraced each other—in this respect I had become totally Persian—and after some congratulatory babbling he said, "You must come now to my father, to pay your respects to the new Prime Minister!"

"Let's have a brief word with Ambassador Henderson before we go. I think he deserves to be told officially, and you are the proper person to do it."

Ardeshir readily agreed, and arm in arm we practically danced along the path to the residence. There we found Loy awaiting us in the garden between his home and the swimming pool. Knowing that our news was good, he had a chilled bottle of champagne ready to greet us. While we told him the news—of Zahedi's triumph, the telegram he had already sent to H.I.M., the make-up of his cabinet—Loy poured us brimming glasses. We toasted the Shah, the new Prime Minister, Dwight Eisenhower, Winston Churchill, and one another. When the bottle was empty, Ardeshir embraced Loy and said he was taking me off to meet the new cabinet. Loy gave a big smile of approval and cheered us on our way.

The Officers' Club was jampacked and riotous with sound. Mustapha and Mohsen were very much in evidence. Everyone, total strangers as well as good friends, embraced me, kissed me on both cheeks—the whole business was happily reminiscent of the night the *firmans* had been delivered from the Caspian to Bill's house.

Finally the new Prime Minister imposed some degree of order. Skipping the German entirely, he made a most kind, grateful speech in Farsi, which was exuberantly translated by Ardeshir.

My response was brief and emphatically explicit on the one important point I wanted to make. I could not resist the temptation to plagiarize, slightly, the great bard himself, William Shakespeare, Francis Bacon, or whoever he may have been.

"Friends, Persians, countrymen, lend me your ears!" I shouted and got a momentary silence. "I thank you for your warmth, your exuberance, your kindness. One thing *must* be clearly understood by all of us. That is, you owe me, the United States, the British, *nothing at all*. We will not, cannot, should not, ask anything from you. Except, if you would like to give them, brief thanks. Those I will accept on behalf of myself, my country and our ally most gratefully.

"Do you understand what I am saying?"

Ardeshir was interpreting my words to his father. They both grinned broadly, gratefully—and I was subjected to a further round of hugging and kissing.

Finally I was able to break away, get back to the Counselor's house and tumble into bed. Having had about two hours' sleep in the last two days, I was lost to the world for at least eighteen hours. One attempt to rouse me was made. The Shah's valet, who had been his classmate in Switzerland many years earlier, was captured in his hiding place by some of Mustapha's young friends. They dragged me downstairs to sit in on his interrogation. Why they suspected him of anything I could not guess and was too dazed to ask. Perhaps because he was hiding; certainly because he was by nature suspicious-looking and evasive-mannered as well. He could not seem to give a straight answer to the simplest question. The interrogation may well have been fascinating, but it could not hold me. I stumbled back to my bed and was sound asleep as I tumbled into it.

And I never remembered to ask what happened to the valet after it was all over.

CHAPTER
13

"His brand, his bow, let no man fear:
The flame, the arrows, all lie here."
Thomas Carew (d. 1638)

Mossadegh was out.
The Shah was in.

It boiled down, quite simply, to that. On Saturday,
August 22 (31 Mordad), His Imperial Majesty the
Shahanshah returned in triumph to the capital city of
his country. Just as my Iranian colleagues earlier had
ruled out any action over the Iranian weekend (Thursday and Friday), so the Shah felt that the kind of
entrance he would be making should not take place
until after the coming weekend was over. On arrival he
was met at Teheran Airport by Prime Minister

Fazlollah Zahedi, all the members of his new cabinet, the entire diplomatic corps and mobs of deliriously happy citizens from all ranks of life. They lined the streets to cheer him as he drove in an open car all the way to Saadabad Palace, north of the city, where the foothills grow into mountains.

This drive, part of which I watched from among the crowd, was a most exhilarating sight, confirmation of what must have been some most exhilarating dreams. I walked back through a swirling, cheering crowd to our embassy on Takht-e-Jamshid, where Ambassador Loy Henderson, most ambassadorially dapper in his cutaway, soon joined me. Mossadegh, he reported, had called a police station and turned himself in the previous evening. What, we wondered, was to be done with him, with General Riahi and others who had betrayed their sovereign? I was to find out the following evening.

Once again, Sunday at midnight, August 23, 1 Shahnivar, I took myself to the palace, this time in an embassy car, this time saluted by the guard who had so carefully ignored me on my previous visits. The driver took me directly to the steps, where a frock-coated aide received me. He bowed low and escorted me up to the second floor, where the Shah was awaiting me in his office and reception room. I had not been there before. H.I.M.'s desk faced into the room from the west, and on the eastern side there were two easy chairs flanking a sofa. Another frock-coated attendant appeared with tiny glasses of vodka and caviar canapés while we were still greeting each other. Then the Shah motioned me to seat myself.

The first words he said were spoken gravely, solemnly. "I owe my throne to God, my people, my army—and to you!" He picked up his glass and raised it, as if in a toast, to me. I raised mine in return, and we both drank. Then he smiled broadly. "It is good to see you here, rather than in an anonymous car on the driveway outside."

I smiled in response. "It *is* good, Your Majesty," I agreed.

"The new Prime Minister, who is now your good friend, as you know, will be coming shortly. Is there anything you would like to discuss before he arrives?"

I hesitated. "Well, sir, I wonder if you have had a chance to make up your mind on what you will do with Mossadegh, Riahi and the others who plotted against you?"

H.I.M. responded decisively. "I have thought much about that. Mossadegh as you know surrendered himself just before my return. He will be sentenced, if the court follows my suggestion"—his lips twitched slightly—"to three years of house arrest in his village. After that he will be free to move about in, but not outside, that village. [Actually, years later, he was allowed to come to Teheran for medical treatment just before his death in the early 1960s.] Riahi will spend three years in jail and will then be released to do as he pleases—*if* what he pleases is not objectionable." Again the slight smile. "A few others will get similar punishment.

"There is one exception. Hossein Fatemi cannot be found yet, but he will be. He was the most vituperative of them all. He urged on the Tudeh gangs that pulled down statues of me and my father. When we find him, he will be executed.

"And your 'friends' the Qashqai khans. You were right about them. I hear that they were in Teheran threatening you. They cannot stay in my country. They will have to go into exile."

I nodded emphatically, in full agreement. "You had better keep an eye on them, Your Majesty, to see that they do not try to sneak back in. They are enemies to be taken seriously."

Another frock coat came silently into the room and whispered a message to the Shahanshah.

"The Prime Minister is here," H.I.M. told me. "Shall we have him in?"

"By all means, sir."

Fazlollah Zahedi was escorted into the chamber, bowed low to H.I.M. and greeted me with a broad, friendly smile.

"Your Majesty," I said formally, "may I repeat to you and your Prime Minister what I said to him and his whole cabinet on Wednesday night?"

The Shah raised his eyebrows in surprise but nodded his approval.

"I told them all, and I repeat this now to Your Majesty, that Iran owes me—us, the Americans and the British who sent me—absolutely nothing. Brief thanks would be received gratefully, but there is no debt, no obligation. We did what we have done to help in our common interest. The outcome is full repayment."

Zahedi smiled again. The Shah gave me a serious look. "We understand. We thank you and will always be grateful. And we will be additionally grateful for your statement that there is no obligation. We accept and understand this fully."

We were all smiles now; warmth and friendship filled the large room. The Shah and Zahedi exchanged a few words in Farsi and then Zahedi took his leave. After he had gone, to my surprise, the Shah reached into his inside jacket pocket and pulled out a large, flat golden cigarette case. Holding it out to me, he asked, "Would you accept this as a souvenir of our recent adventure?"

I stammered my thanks and stuffed it into my coat

pocket. If I'd been dressed as I was for our earlier meetings, I'd have had no place to put it. A few minutes later, H.I.M. personally escorted me down the stairway and out to the palace steps.

"Come," he said, "I want to introduce you to a friend of yours whom you have not yet met."

Below us, on the bottom step, stood a proud figure.

"As I told you, I plan few punishments. And I have made only one promotion. I present you now to *General* Nassiry!"

The burly officer saluted smartly. To me he looked like a giant.

Loy Henderson was still up awaiting me when I reached the residence, although it was well after one o'clock in the morning.

"Have a good time?" he asked cheerfully.

I pulled the gold case out of my pocket. "Look at what H.I.M. gave me."

Loy reached out and took it from me. "It's a beauty." He snapped it open and looked inside. "I've got a suggestion. Why don't you let me take it back the next time I have an audience and ask the Shah if he will have his name and the date engraved here?" He pointed to the flat inner surface opposite the clip which held the cigarettes in place.

"That's a great idea, Loy. I'd be most grateful if you'd do that."

"And now let me tell you how you are leaving, Mr. 'Scar on Right Forehead.'" The Ambassador had been amused at the way my entrance to Iran had been recorded. "This time there will be no trace at all of your border crossing. The naval attaché, who has the only airplane that the embassy can use, will pick you up here and will fly you to Bahrein tomorrow morning. A Military Air Transport Service plane—neither pilots nor passengers knowing your identity—will take you aboard and leave you in Beirut. I've booked you in true name on a BOAC flight to London and am asking our embassy there to notify the Foreign Office of your arrival time. About an hour ago Ardeshir called to ask when and how you are leaving. He will be at the airport to see you off."

With that we parted company. Presumably Loy slept well. I know that I did not. Thoughts and memories of the recent past were racing through my head. They would continue to do so for some time to come.

The naval attaché arrived at what seemed to me an inordinately early hour and took me to a special section of the field where private and small official planes were hangared. Mustapha and Ardeshir were already waiting there. Ardeshir also had a parting present for me. It turned out to be another gold cigarette case, thicker but shorter than the Shah's gift. (It held ten, H.I.M.'s twenty, cigarettes. Clearly I had been smoking far too much on this Teheran visit.) He made a little, rather formal, speech of gratitude. Then the customary Persian embrace dissolved the formality. I stumbled onto the airplane with tears in my eyes. The flight to Bahrein is a complete blank in my memory.

But I do remember landing, taxiing up close beside the large MATS plane, saying goodbye to the naval attaché and joining the puzzled crew and passengers who were to accompany me to Beirut. Once there I waited till the passengers had disembarked, then I walked with the crew into the terminal building, which I knew well. I avoided the immigration officers and went directly to the BOAC booth. It never crossed my mind that I might have to pay for my ticket—I don't think I had enough cash to do so—but it was all right. I had a first-class passage to London, and there was a message for me. Gordon Somerset would meet me on my arrival.

Again, I have no memories of the flight to London. We must have landed a couple of times, perhaps in Athens and Rome. At Heathrow Airport Gordon had used official prerogative—he had told the Foreign Office the whole story—to board the airplane before we disembarked. He whisked me through immigration and customs control and carted me off, in an official limousine with a uniformed chauffeur, to the Ritz Hotel. This was the height of the tourist season. All Foreign Office had been able to get me was a tiny room, barely large enough to contain a single bed, one chair, a coat rack and a washbasin. Gordon explained apologetically, but I scarcely heard him. He did say that he would pick me up at ten the next morning, take me to see Mr. Cochran, then for lunch with Henry Montague, when I could give them all the gory details of my experience, and after that to 10 Downing Street to see the Prime Minister. Eden, I gathered, was out of the country; Churchill was recovering from a stroke but most anxious to see me. I mumbled thanks, pushed him out the door, shucked off my clothing and fell onto the bed. There I slept like the proverbial log for ten hours and awoke feeling considerably refreshed, almost human. Breakfast, with a pot of strong tea, scrambled eggs and that decidedly noncrisp British bacon, also helped. By the time Gordon arrived to pick me up, I was quite alert, ready to go.

And we went. I had my routine down cold, in living color, with much praise for Nossey and Cafron, but a request that the British refrain from contacting them for the time being and *no* mention of the Boscoe brothers. I did name the officers that Peter Stoneman had recruited—the "Dancing Master" and the "Young Turks"—and I also said that General Guilanshah had been a most valuable ally. I observed that we proved to have one agent in common, the one we called "Rosencrantz," who had been most valuable in handling communications with the palace. The meeting with Cochran went extremely well. He was warm and congratulatory.

Next I joined Henry Montague, Gordon and a couple of other senior staff members for a long lunch. They wanted the whole story, all the names and numbers of the players, every suspicion, hope or anxiety I had known. They took me to the Grill Room of the Connaught Hotel, perhaps the best and most expensive place in London, so I assumed Cochran must have authorized it as a business expense. Anyhow, when the bill came Henry took an envelope from his pocket, gave a fifty-pound note to the waiter and put what change he got, after a substantial tip, back into the envelope. The quiz was exhaustive, but my story of agents was accepted without suspicion. Mostly, what they wanted was a full account, concentrating on the glamorous features of the operation. Much of it was familiar to them from my cables, which Henry Montague had transmitted to London and Washington from Cyprus. They knew the story of Princess Ashraf and General Schwarzkopf, my first meetings with H.I.M. and the disastrous failure of "Rosencrantz" to deliver the *firmans* to the Shah in time. But from that moment on I had communicated little. It was this gap in their knowledge that I must now fill in—and I did, as elaborately and excitingly as I possibly could. By the time I reached 10 Downing Street I would have it all down cold.

So I gave in glamorous detail the story of what happened after Nassiry's deliverance of the *firman* to Mossadegh and his arrest by General Riahi. The assembling of our refugees, including Nossey, Cafron,

Mustapha and Mohsen, the reproduction of that *firman* and the one appointing Zahedi as Prime Minister in his place, the efforts of Mustapha and Mohsen to raise military support from Isfahan and Kermanshah, the glorious rising of 28 Mordad and, finally, the appearance of General Guilanshah with his clattering tanks, overloaded with cheering soldiers, to take Zahedi in triumph to the Officers' Club—by now I was sure I could tell the story in my sleep. Soon I was to find out if I could tell it to someone else in *his* sleep.

Eventually the lunch, and my story, came to an end. The party dispersed. I was placed in the car that had met me at the airport, with the same driver, but without Gordon, and I was driven to Number 10 Downing Street. Another climactic moment was approaching.

At precisely four o'clock I rang the doorbell. A military aide, a lieutenant colonel, let me in.

"Mr. Roosevelt? Come this way, please."

He led me to a downstairs room, a living room, I guessed, that had been made into a bedroom. Churchill, whom I had not seen since the White House Christmas party of 1941, was lying, propped up by pillows, in the middle of the bed. He waved and grunted a greeting. A stroke had confined him thus for the last month. The aide seated me close by him, but on his left, and then withdrew.

"Stupid idiot," Churchill grumbled. "He should know I can't hear a thing with my left ear. Move over to the other side, will you?"

I picked up the chair, carried it around to his right and sat down again.

"We met at your cousin Franklin's, did we not? I thought so. Well, you have an exciting story to tell. I'm anxious to hear it."

So I went into my routine, leaving out any discussion of agents—he couldn't care less about them—but giving him the dramatic highlights in considerable detail. Quite often he interrupted with questions, and quite often he would doze off for a few minutes. He was, it seemed, consumed alternately by curiosity and by sleepiness.

We talked for almost two hours. When I found him snoozing briefly, I simply repeated what I had been saying as soon as I had his attention again. He was fascinated with the account of my early meetings with the Shah and with the reasoning which had led H.I.M. to fly to Baghdad after Mossadegh's radio speech on the early morning of August 16. He was also intrigued by the activities of the Qashqai.

"Never could trust those damned Qashqai. They screwed us up in World War One as well as in World War Two. A treacherous bunch. You were wise to discourage H.I.M. from going to Shiraz."

I described the Islamic tradition stemming from the Hegira and how the Shah and I had discussed it.

"Strategic withdrawal," he grunted. "Mohammed was a smart chap. And Mohammed Reza Shah Pahlavi has his smarts too." He dozed away once more.

When he woke up again I described my final meeting with the Shah, the bringing in of Prime Minister Zahedi and my emphatic statement that they must not consider themselves in any way obligated to us. At this point Churchill was hardly overwhelmed with enthusiasm, but he raised no objection. Finally I quoted the Shah's words about owing his country to God and some others, including me. Churchill grinned and shifted himself further up on his pillows.

"Young man," he said, "if I had been but a few years younger, I would have loved nothing better than to have served under your command in this great venture!"

"Thank you, sir" was all I could say to what was, coming from this man, *the* supreme compliment.

I winged my way back across the Atlantic with one more meeting to face, one more report to deliver.

But first I would go to Nantucket to catch the last few days of August with my family on that lovely island.

Now I was reviewing my memory of how AJAX had been approved, of what the Dulles brothers and their boss, President Dwight Eisenhower, might be expected to remember and what I should have to provide in explanation of what had finally happened.*

"Ike," I recalled, had first met the Shah while he was still president of Columbia University and had concluded that he would prove "an effective leader of his people." Soon after that, before he had moved to Washington to take office, Mossadegh sent him a long cable explaining why, in his opinion, the U.S. should support his expropriation of AIOC. The President-elect stated his impartiality in reply. On May 28, about a month before the meeting in JFD's office which authorized me to act, Mossadegh sent another long message asking for help in removing obstacles to the sale of Iranian oil, or, if that were impossible, aiding Iran to develop other resources. A month later Ike replied: It was up to the Iranian government to decide its own best interests, *but* failure to agree with the British on oil compensation would make it unthinkable that the U.S. should buy Iranian oil. Soon after that I was on my way.

I was still unbelievably sleepy. Most of the way to New York I was dozing. Once there, I pulled myself together enough to find a flight to Nantucket and to telephone my wife that I was on my way.

On Friday, September 4, 1953, I reported at the

---

*Eisenhower recounted his understanding of the affair in *Mandate for Change, 1953–1956,* published in 1963 by Doubleday & Company, New York. Pages 159–166 cover the whole story as Eisenhower knew it. He quotes but does not name me.

White House to President Eisenhower, the two Dulles brothers, Secretary of Defense Wilson (one of the few—in addition to the brothers, Loy Henderson and of course myself—who had actually supported the operation at the June meeting in JFD's office), Admiral Radford, Chairman of the Joint Chiefs of Staff, and General Andy Goodpastor.* Now, at home base, I was better equipped to illustrate my report than I ever had been—even in Teheran. An easel was set up to hold maps and charts—a map of Iran; of Teheran; of the road from the Iraqi frontier through Kermanshah, Hamadan and Kasvin to Teheran, by which I had entered Iran and which Tahuyi had taken to get the support of the colonel in Kermanshah; of the Caspian coast, where the Shah had waited for word, and Tabriz, which had come out for the Shah on the early morning of August 19 (28 Mordad); and of Isfahan, where Mustapha had sought in vain for military help, to Shiraz, the "capital" of the Qashqai. The charts gave the strength of the different military units in Teheran, Kermanshah and Isfahan, population figures for the major cities and much other, generally irrelevant, information.

However, the substance of my report had nothing new; it was simply a combination of what I had told our British allies and the story I had given to the dozing Winston Churchill. It was, I thought, very well received. In fact one of my audience seemed almost alarmingly enthusiastic. John Foster Dulles was leaning back in his chair. Despite his posture, he was anything but sleepy. His eyes were gleaming; he seemed to be purring like a giant cat. Clearly, he was not only enjoying what he was hearing, but my instincts told me that he was planning as well. What was in his mind I could not guess. Would it be a future

*Who has now returned from retirement to command at West Point.

employment of the same counterrevolutionary—or revolutionary—approach? So I closed my presentation on a warning note.

"Gentlemen, there is one thing I want to make very clear. We were successful in this venture because our assessment of the situation in Iran *was* correct. We believed—and we were proven right—that if the people and the armed forces were shown that they must choose, that Mossadegh was forcing them to choose, between their monarch and a revolutionary figure backed by the Soviet Union, they could, and would, make only one choice. With some help from us, but mostly because Mossadegh, the Tudeh and eventually the U.S.S.R. itself, forced the choice upon them, the populace made a choice. And most convincingly. The people and the army came, overwhelmingly, to the support of the Shah. You can have no idea from here—you really had to be in Iran—of the heartfelt strength of that support.

"If our analysis had been wrong, we'd have fallen flat on our, er, faces. But it was right.

"If we, the CIA, are ever going to try something like this again, we must be absolutely sure that people and army want what we want.

"If not, you had better give the job to the Marines!"

But Foster Dulles did not want to hear what I was saying. He was still leaning back in his chair with a catlike grin on his face. Within weeks I was offered command of a Guatemalan undertaking already in preparation. A quick check suggested that my requirements were not likely to be met. I declined the offer. Later, I resigned from the CIA—before the Bay of Pigs disaster underlined the validity of my warning.

INDEX

INDEX

Catalog

If you are interested in a list of fine Paperback
books, covering a wide range of subjects
and interests, send your name and address,
requesting your free catalog, to:

McGraw-Hill Paperbacks
1221 Avenue of Americas
New York, N.Y. 10020